PEARL HARBOR

Copyright Library of Congress-in-Publication Data
Cooper,Shannon 1961-
Remembering Pearl Harbor: How we Servred and survived December 7th 1941/MS2 Shannon R. Cooper,USNR (Ret.)
P. cm
Includes index
ISSN 979-888680498-0 (Softcover binding:50# alkaline paper
Pearl (Hawaii), Attack on,1941-Personal narratives.
World War, 1937-1945- Personal narratives, American.
United States-Armed Forces-Biography.
Oral History-United States.
Title
British Library cataloging data are available

Cover design by Daniel Lopez contracted through Fiverr.
Front cover photo provided with permission from History on the Net.
Back cover photo was taken by Melvin McCullough Jr.
Manufactured in the United States of America.

PEARL HARBOR

MS2 SHANNON R. COOPER USNR (RET.)

TABLE OF CONTENTS

BOOK DISCLAIMER

Some material in this book may contain actions or words that may offend certain people. It is not the intention of the author to bully, discriminate or insult any race, sex, or religion of any person. This is a book used to enlighten, educate, and show respect to all that were involved in the Pearl Harbor attack. Keep in mind this was in a totally different time and generation. Times have definitely changed since 1941. Please view it with discretion.

Written by Shannon R. Cooper

DEDICATION

This book is dedicated to all who paid the ultimate sacrifice with their lives given in the service of their country.

On Sunday, December 7, 1941, eighty-one years ago, the United States Naval Base in Pearl Harbor, Hawaii was brutally attacked by the empire of Japan.

Let us not forget their stories and the survivors' stories. Let us all honor their legacy.

By MS2 Shannon R. Cooper, U.S.N.R. (Retired)

ACKNOWLEDGEMENTS

First and foremost, I would like to thank all the military men and women who shared their Pearl Harbor memories and experiences with me on my journey of discovery on the subject of Pearl Harbor, December 7, 1941.

I humbly want to express gratitude and much needed respect to all that perished on December 7, 1941. Military, both men and women, civilians, and children. May God Bless you all. For all that paid the Ultimate sacrifice, thank you!

I want to thank The NavSource for all their help and information provided for this book.

I would like to thank the History Channel and the Managing Editor of History on the Net and his Podcast called Eyewitness History.

I also would love to send a thanks and love to my veteran brothers and sisters especially Our Training officer Ronee Jordan, USAF. at American Legion Post 226 in Coweta, Oklahoma. On December 2021 during our Post meeting Ronee Jordan conducted training on the subject of Pearl Harbor. Afterwards I was truly inspired to write this book as a fundraiser and to share the survivor`s stories to local school kids .

I want to acknowledge the love of my life, my wife, Sandy Craig Cooper. She always supports me in all and every aspect of my life. I could not have written this book without your support!

I want to give a special thanks to my friend, editor and mentor, Linda Hight, an avid and accomplished writer. I would have not been able to complete this book without her guidance.

Thank you all.

INTRODUCTION

This book is written to honor the survivors of the attack on our country in Pearl Harbor on December 7, 1941. Some of the stories are written from the perspective of a young child as a result of an assignment given while attending school. Other stories are written by the families of those who survived the Pearl Harbor attack.

To remember and to honor those soldiers, sailors and airmen for all their sacrifices is of utmost importance.

We are obligated to pass on the stories of those who survived this attack. It is time to tell the whole story which includes not only the Americans, but the Japanese.

You will be there as these survivors and their families tell their stories to the next generation and the two sides of the story will be talked about by the survivors. Their stories will help us gain more understanding of what really happened and why the actions were taken on December 7, 1941.

THE AUTHOR'S STORY

This is my membership acknowledgement. This is in no way an endorsement of this book.

THIS IS MY STORY

AUTHOR - SHANNON RAY COOPER

I joined the United States Navy in 1979 while I was still attending high school at Tokay High School in Lodi, California. I signed up under the Delayed Entry Program (DEP). This program allows students to sign up and be sworn in prior to graduation.

I attended Boot Camp at Naval Recruit Training Center in San Diego, California in October 1980. I was asked to be in a special company while in Boot Camp called the Crack Rifle Drill Team. The training for this special company required a lot more training and practicing belonging to this team. We woke up an hour before everyone else to practice drilling. Plus, we still had to train and march and learn what the rest of the Boot Camp companies learned as well. My only regret was the fact that my parents were unable to attend by graduation from Boot Camp.

After Boot Camp, I was off to my "A" school to learn my job (Rating) in the Navy. My school was located at the Balboa Navy Hospital Training Facility in San Diego, California.

After nineteen weeks of training, it was off to Field Medical Training Battalion at Camp Pendleton, California. We were taught how to be a Combat Medic for the United States Marine Corps. The training lasted for approximately eight weeks. After the training, I was allowed to take thirty days leave (vacation) and I got to spend time with my family.

My first Duty Station was the U.S.S. Barbour County LST-1195. It was a tank leading ship that performed amphibious operations with the United States Marine Corps, Land, Sea and Air. I obtained the rank of E-3 HMSN Hospital Corpsman Seaman.

I was first assigned to the Ship's Medical Department Sick Call Unit. I was only attached to the Marine Corps during amphibious operations. I found it was extremely hard to advance in rank as a Hospital Corpsman. The one thing about being on a ship is that everyone has to do temporary duty in the mess hall and galley for a period of ninety days. Well, I got my turn.

Most sailors dreaded the ninety-day temporary duty in the mess hall and galley. I, on the other hand, absolutely loved it.

When the time came to take by E-4 exam, I studied and passed the Mess Management Specialists (Cook), Third Class Petty Officer Advancement Exam. I cross-rated from HM to MS.

I learned my new job by getting" on the job training." I learned to cook from the Navy's best cooks in the fleet.

On May 10, 1982, we sailed north towards Bremerton, Washington to participate in Armed Forces Day celebrations. We moved alongside the Battleship U.S.S. Missouri BB-63 and saw she was being mothballed. This was my first experience with the Missouri. They were giving tours of the decks during daylight hours. Since I was a cook who worked sixteen-hour shifts, I never got an official tour. After hours, I took a self-guided tour of her massive, teak wood decks. The first time I set foot on the Missouri, it was love at first sight. I remember saying, "What a beautiful ship you are. I would have loved serving on you."

Pearl Harbor

I still have memories of the first time I went to Pearl Harbor, Hawaii when our ship went on a Northern-Pacific cruise in August 1982. While enroute from San Diego, California to Hawaii, our ship rescued three people from a sinking sailboat.

Upon entering Pearl Harbor for the first time, I had such feelings of pride, respect and patriotism. At the same time, there was a sad and humble side as I manned the side of our ship to render honors to the U.S.S. Arizona BB-39 Memorial.

After dropping off the survivors from the sailboat in Hawaii, our ship embarked as surveillance personnel for an intelligence gathering mission to Petropavlovsk-Kamchatka which is a city in Russia. The U.S.S. Barbour County steamed into the norther Pacific and conducted two weeks of special operations off Kamchatka between August 23rd and September 7. Following a short break in September, during which we visited Adak and Attu in the Aleutians, surveillance operations were finished on September 28. During this cruise, the crew sighted numerous Soviet submarines, aircraft and surface warships. We returned to San Diego, California via Seattle, Washington on October 17. Aside from a short period of Amphibious Refresher Training in early December, the rest of the year was spent in port.

On January 30, 1983, the U.S.S. Barbour County deployed to the western Pacific in the company with New Orleans (LPH-11), Durham (LKA-114, Schenectady (LST-1185) and Denver (LPD-9). After stopping in Hawaii for two days of boat exercises, the unit crossed the Pacific and arrived in Subic Bay in the Philippines on February 22. While in port there on March 1, the U.S.S. Barbour County suffered a small fire that damaged the degaussing cables. A Damage Control Party from Hull (DD-945) helped the tank landing ship's crew put out the fire.

On July7, 1983, I left active duty. I moved to Silsbee, Texas to live with my Dad, Bobby Ray Cooper, my sister, Mashell Cooper and my Stepmom, Sue Cooper. I got married on December 12, 1983. Our daughter, Carrie, was born on April 30, 1984. I stayed active in the Navy Reserve and drilled in Orange, Texas.

In August 1984, I was doing my active duty for training in San Diego, California. My wife, Susan, moved to Phoenix, Arizona to provide emotional support for her dad after the loss of his wife. Her dad was a Navy veteran. When I finished my active duty for training, I met up with my wife and daughter in Arizona. We stayed there and I worked various odd jobs as an armed armored car officer, armed alarm response officer and floor maintenance worker. On May 6, 1985, our son, Brandon, was born.

While serving in the Navy Reserves in Phoenix, they asked for volunteers to go back on active duty to serve on one of the four Iowa class battleships. I jumped at the opportunity to put in for duty on the U.S.S. Missouri BB-63. In order to be considered for duty, there was an extensive background check and you had to obtain great evaluation marks along with two letters of recommendation. I had gotten a letter from the Commanding Officer of Barbour County CDR, John Donnelly. I also got a letter from Rear Admiral Horne. I finally got the good news that I got selected for duty. My wife did not share my enthusiasm.

In June 1985, I reported for duty once again to Recruit Training Center/Naval Training Center, San Diego, California. For two weeks, I went through the NAVET program. This was a program to re-acclimate the reservist to active duty. You are re-issued a new set of full uniforms. We marched everywhere.

Upon graduation, you are authorized to wear the rank of Second-Class Petty Officer. I did take my advancement exam while in the reserves. We were assigned to live temporarily on a floating barge located outside Long Beach Naval Shipyard.

The U.S.S. Missouri was towed by tugboats from Bremerton, Washington to Long Beach, California Naval Shipyard. We were the pre-commission crew. When we got the chance to visit the U.S.S. Missouri, she was in dry dock. It was like seeing an old friend once again. She was an amazing and remarkable thing to see. I was now part of her history.

The shipyard and the Navy removed all the obsolete weaponry and equipment and gave her a total make-over. Our crew got the opportunity to help work on and assist the shipyard workers restore the U.S.S. Missouri back to her former glory.

In February 1986, we departed for sea trials. On May 10, 1986, our ship entered San Francisco Bay for its re-commissioning ceremony. The sleeping giant once again heard the call to arms. There were a few VIPs in attendance. They included Defense Secretary Caspar W. Weinberger, Navy Secretary John Lehman, Margaret Truman and California Governor John Ashcroft. Defense Secretary Caspar W. Weinberger called it "a day to celebrate the rebirth of American sea power after years of dangerous neglect." He also said, "Listen to the footsteps of those who have gone before. So far, the echo of those footsteps has led us to proudly and prestigiously march wherever the ship has taken us."

Defense Secretary Weinberger called the 887.5-foot battleship which had been modernized with a budget cost of $475 million a key part of President Reagan's plan to bring our Navy's strength up to six hundred ships. He said, "The re-commissioning was one of the greatest satisfactions of my tenure." San Francisco's Mayor Dianne Feinstein, who fought a political battle to have the ship home-ported there, called the re-commissioning "a profound statement for peace."

In September 1986, we departed Long Beach, California which was the start of our world cruise. It was our mission to again circumnavigate the world as President Roosevelt's "Great White Fleet" had done. In September 1986, we crossed the Equator and the International Date Line which is located near Australia. We went through the Golden Shellback initiation. We visited Sydney, Australia and participated in the Royal Australian Navy's 75th Anniversary celebrations. Other ports we visited included Diego Garcia, Egypt, Turkey, Italy, Spain, Portugal, Panama and Suez Canal. We returned to our home port on December 19, 1986.

On July 7, 1986, my tour of duty was over. I moved to Las Vegas, Nevada. I joined the Culinary Union. I really thought they would send me out on a cooking job with all my Navy cooking experience. I was wrong.

I was hired as a dishwasher and did every job there was in a kitchen for the next six years. They said I had to pay my dues and earn the privilege to be a cook.

I stayed active in the Navy Reserves. In August 1990, I completed a ninety-day tour of Desert Shield as Relief Personnel. In January 1991, I completed two tours in Desert Storm. In August 1991, I was honorably discharged from the Navy Duty Reserve.

I continued to work part-time as a cook. In 2001, my family and I lost our home in a fire where we lost everything. That same year, I was hired at the Paris Las Vegas Hotel Casino as a Security Officer. They offered to pay for the Emergency Medical Technician (EMT) training given by American Medical Response. I worked as an EMT for twenty-one years in Las Vegas, Nevada.

In 2009, I moved to Okmulgee, Oklahoma for a job as a Corrections Officer. That year, I had a heart attack and could not return to a stressful job.

I then completed Certified Nursing Assistant (CAN) training. In 2010, I had another massive heart attack and had triple bypass surgery.

In 2014, I worked at Oklahoma State University (OSU) as a Chef. I retired in 2016 from OSU and then met the love of my life, Sandy Craig Tomak.

In 2016, Sandy went into the hospital with phenomena. She was in the Intensive Care Unit for forty-five days and I stayed by her bedside the entire time. When she came out of sedation, I proposed to her. We were married on July 1, 2016.

I am a member of the American Legion Post 226 in Coweta, Oklahoma.

1937 TO 1941

Prior to the surprise attack on Pearl Harbor on December 7, 1941, the United States and Japan had not been on exactly friendly terms for decades.

The United States was not particularly happy with the way Japan treated China. The Japanese government felt it was in their best interest to solve its economic and demographic problems by expanding into China's territory. By doing this, they dominated the import market.

In 1937, Japan declared war on the Republic of China. This resulted in the Nanjing Massacre or Battle on December 13, 1937. Nanjing was the capital of The Republic of China during part of the Ming dynasty. This was random murder, wartime rape, looting and arson on a massive scale. It was all against the civilians of Nanjing and lasted for six weeks with an estimated death toll of approximately 300,000 deaths. It was looked upon clearly as war crimes against China.

The response from the United States to Japan's aggression towards China was to put in place severe economic sanctions and trade embargoes on oil and gas. Japan did not handle this action well.

Retaliation was inevitable. In August 1940, President Roosevelt provided China with financial aid to help fund their war effort.

On September 27, 1940, Japan aligned with Germany and Italy which was called the Axis.

In March of 1941, the United States and the Japanese government began a series of diplomatic discussions. These discussions took place in Washington, DC.

On July 26, 1941, President Roosevelt took action by freezing Japan's assets. The United States government and the Japanese government failed to avert war. Their efforts were unsuccessful. The United States government suspected that Japan might attack the United States. The peace talks between the United States and Japan ended in August of 1941.

WORLD WAR II SPIES WHO HELPED THE JAPANESE GOVERNMENT

These spies lived in Hawaii in 1941. This information was gathered and adapted from former top secret, now declassified FBI files.

By MS2 Shannon R. Cooper, U.S.N.R.

Former German Naval Officer, Bernard Julius Otto Kuehn and his family were spies. They were hired by the Abwehr. The Abwehr was an organization that was primarily responsible for military intelligence in Germany from 1921 to 1944. They worked for Nazi Germany and had ties with Propaganda Minister Joseph Goebbels.

In 1935 Goebbels offered Dr. Bernard Kuehn a job working with the Japanese intelligence in Hawaii. Kuehn accepted the job and moved his family to Honolulu, Hawaii on August 15,1935.

His family included Dr. Bernard Kuehn who was forty-one years old, his wife, Fredel and daughter Suzie who was seventeen years old. Also, his eleven-year-old son, Hans Joachim.

The entire Kuehn family played their part in the family spying operation. They were all involved in espionage. They were referred to as the "eight- eyed spy." Daughter Suzie would go on dates with members of the military stationed there in Pearl Harbor. She able to get important information on the movement of Navy ships and day to day operations.

Suzie also worked a different angle on intelligence gathering of information. She opened a beauty parlor there in Honolulu, Hawaii. She was smart and offered the cheapest prices in town. She would target the wives and girlfriends of high-ranking officers. Those women sure liked to gossip. They wanted to talk so much that Suzie couldn't wait for them to leave.

Her brother, Hahns at only 11 years old was trained by his father how to spy and how to ask all the right questions about both ships and submarines. Every morning Bernard would have his son dress up in a U.S. Navy sailor suit to project the image of patriotism. They would both go for walks by the water's edge. The Navy Officers would see Hahns all dressed up and invite him to come aboard their ships and submarines. That is when he started spying and getting some crucial information.

Bernard's wife's role was to gather all the information gathered from her spying family and keep a record of all the intelligence they had learned.

On March 27, 1941, Former Japanese Naval officer, now master spy Takeo Yoshikawa, arrived in Oahu, Hawaii. He was portraying himself as Tadashi Morimura, the new Japanese Vice Consul with Nagao Kita the new Japanese Consul arriving on board the Liner Nitta Maru. Because of all of Yoshikawa's experience in the Japanese Navy and his knowledge of the U.S. Navy, he was a valuable asset to the spying operation there at Pearl Harbor.

He rented a second story apartment that overlooked Pearl Harbor. He would often check out Oahu and learn the layout of the land just to get himself familiar with his surroundings. He was keeping notes on the Navy fleets coming and goings and security measures.

He rented small planes at John Rodgers Airport and flew around the island to observe all the U.S. military instillations, taking note of locations and distance from the harbor. He dove in the harbor using a hollow reed to breath with and rode on a Navy's tugboat. On the tugboat, he listened carefully to any and all the gossip about Navy movement and operations.

He worked closely with German spy Bernard Kuehn and also untrained spy Seki Koichi. Seki served as the Consulate's treasurer. According to Yoshikawa, there were over 160,000 people of Japanese descent who occupied Hawaii during 1941. Yoshikawa at this time was not informed about plans to attack Pearl harbor. He just thought it would be great information of any future attack.

A large number of Japanese were loyal to the Hawaiian people. Most felt unworthy in their presence and would not have betrayed them.

Yoshikawa would send all his intelligence information transmitted by the Japanese Consulate in PURPLE code to the Foreign Ministry, which then forwarded the information to the Japanese Navy. Little did Japan know their code had been broken by Allied code breakers. All messages to and from Tokyo were intercepted and decoded.

One particular message was addressed to Kita for Yoshikawa sent on September 24, 1941, should have received more attention than it did. It was a diagram that divided Pearl Harbor into five distinct zones and requested the location and number of U.S. Navy ships in port. Due to the delays brought about by staff shortages, this message was overlooked.

Japan's Admiral Isoroku Yamamoto finalized his plan for attack on Pearl Harbor. Bernard reported to Yoshikawa all the intelligence gathered by his family. Bernard would send coded messages that were not always of good value.

At first, Bernard was not very detectable by American intelligence. He would flash coded messages from his attic and flashing a light. This brought the attention of Americans. Bernard was under suspicion by the F.B.I. due to his affiliation to the Nazi party.

On February 21, 1942, just seventy-six days after the Pearl Harbor attack, Benard Julius Otto Kuehn was found guilty of spying. He was sentenced to be shot by Musketry in Honolulu. However, he ended up serving a long prison sentence.

Kuehn and his family were released and deported back to Germany. All this information was available thanks to the Freedom of Information Act. Also, Japan's National Information Discloser law including Right to information Act.

PREFACE
JAPANESE PLAN FOR ATTACK

by MS2 Shannon R. Cooper, MS2 USNR-(Ret.)

In January 1941, Japan's Admiral Isoroku Yamamoto was instrumental in a master plan to execute a sneak attack on the United States (U.S.) Naval Base at Pearl Harbor, Hawaii. This was eleven months prior to the actual attack on December 7, 1941.

His goal was to cripple and destroy the U.S. Navy fleet. Specifically, the Navy's carriers and battleships. With the U.S. Navy fleet out of the way, they posed no threat to Japan's domination of all of Asia.

At the same time, German Chancellor Adolf Hitler held a conference with his Generals to plan to attack the Soviet Union. Hitler knew that a successful attack on Russia would motivate Japan to attack the United States. This would also distract the U.S. from getting involved in war in the United Kingdom.

The Japanese set out a precise and carefully executed attack on the U.S. Navy Fleet. This took several months of intense planning and training.

On the early morning hours on November 26, 1941, the Japanese Navy departed their homeland of Japan, going forth in their war plan of attack on the United States, specifically Pearl Harbor, Hawaii. This was all conditional of the outcome of Japan and U.S. peace negotiations. If they were successful then Japan would abort their attack and act of war, and simply return back to their homeland.

Negotiations had been ongoing for months. Japan was wanting the U.S. to end the economic sanctions that were imposed upon Japan. However, both parties were at a deadlock, and neither would budge.

The Japanese task force consisted of six of Japan's first line aircraft carriers, Akagi, Kaga, Soryu, Hiryu, Shokaku, and Zuikaku. They carried all the Japanese Zero War planes which was a total of four hundred twenty aircraft. This was the most powerful carrier task force displayed. This also included battleships, cruisers, and escort destroyers. The task force traveled a total of 3,150 nautical miles to get within striking distance towards Pearl Harbor, Hawaii. This took Japan only eleven days to get into striking distance of Pearl Harbor.

At 0545 hours (5:45 A.M.) the task force gave their last briefing to all the pilots. This also helped encourage and motivate their pilots prior to going into battle. Japan is extremely patriotic and dedicated to Japan. At 0610 hours (6:10 A.M.) the first Japanese wave of planes made up of 131 Aichi 3A2, Val Type 99, Mitsubishi A6M2 Zeke or Zero model11, 143 NakajimaB5N2 Kate Type 97, Model 12 Single engine torpedo bombers.

Due to the shallow waters in Pearl Harbor, the torpedoes had to be modified with wooden rudders.

There were two waves of attack planned. The first wave of one hundred eighty-three fighter planes arrived in skies above Pearl Harbor at 0755 hours (7:55A.M.) The second wave had one hundred seventy planes and attacked at 0854 hours (8:54 A.M.)

THE ATTACK
CHRONOLOGY OF THE ATTACK

The Chronology Of The Attack is historically recorded by both eyewitness reports and, also from The Deck Logs Of The U.S. Navy Ships which were moored at Pearl Harbor on December 7, 1941.

The following is an accurate historical account of the chain of events that took place on that fateful day provided by Navsource Naval History.

It was 6:18 A.M. local Hawaiian time. On the morning December 7, 1941, Task Force 8 Included these U.S. Navy Ships: Enterprise, Northampton, Salt Lake City, Chester, (Crudiv 5), Dunlap, Eliot, Fanning, Benham, Gridley, Maury and the Balch (Desron 6). They were returning to Pearl Harbor after completing their mission in the vicinity of Wake Island which is located in the Western Pacific ocean.

From a position of approximately two hundred fifteen nautical miles west of Pearl Harbor, routing scouting flights are launched. They had orders to search a specific sector for distance of one hundred fifty nautical miles.

The planes then proceeded to Pearl Harbor. Three military aircraft were also launched to establish inner air patrol. The U.S.S. Antares (AKS-

3), an auxiliary ship, arrived off Pearl Harbor from Canton and Palmyra with five hundred tons steel barge in tow.

They sighted a suspicious object fifteen hundred yards on the starboard quarter. It appeared to be a small submarine, but they could not positively identify it. Accordingly, they notified inshore patrol ship, Ward, to investigate it.

6:33 A.M. the Antares observed a Navy Patrol plane that circled and dropped two smoke pots near the object.

6:45 A.M. Antares observed the U.S.S. Ward (DD-483) commence firing for two minutes at enemy contact. A patrol plane appeared to drop bombs or depth charged objects which disappeared.

7:00 A.M. VP Squadron 24, an anti- submarine patrol, had four of the six planes depart Pearl Harbor for scheduled training exercise in operating area C-5. The other two planes were out of commission as one needed structural change and the other plane was in standby status for ready duty.

One of the planes in the squadron sank one enemy submarine that was one mile from the entrance to Pearl Harbor.

Forces were disposed around Pearl Harbor with 50% of the aircraft on four hours' notice. Specific duty assignments required six planes to be ready for flight on just thirty minutes notice.

All planes had to be ready for flight or in the air in four hours or less. There were seventy-two planes.

When the first bomb dropped, fourteen patrol aircraft were in the air with seven on search from Midway. A total of fifty-eight planes were ready for flight in four hours or less. Nine were undergoing repairs.

7:02 A.M. two U.S. Army enlisted men, U.S. Army Private George Elliott Jr. and Private Joeseph Lockard, were on duty at Opana radar site located at Kahuku Point on Northern Oahu, Hawaii. In 1941 radar technology was still in the infancy stage of development and was new to all. The two men had gone through training and were operating a SCR-270 model radar.

Elliott spotted something completely out of the ordinary on the radar screen which appeared as a huge blip approximately one hundred thirty-seven miles out. Elliott immediately called headquarters and reported this information to nearby information center at Fort Shafter. He was initially told there was nobody on duty to take the information. Elliott waited for a call back, which came minutes later.

Lockard took the call and told the Duty Officer, Army Lieutenant Kermit Tyler, that the radar blips were an unusually large flight approaching. In fact, he commented that it was the largest he had ever seen on the equipment. Tyler responded that what Lockard was seeing were American B-17 bombers flying to Pearl Harbor from the Mainland. "Don't worry about it," Tyler told Lockard.

The two soldiers continued to track the blip which grew so large that Lockard thought the radar was broken. They turned off the radar at 0745 7:45 A.M. after the blip fell behind the Oahu's mountains.

Message alert at 7:40 A.M. came that the United States sank an enemy submarine one mile from Pearl Harbor. At 7:40 A.M. Patron 21 staff duty officer C-C was informed of the patrol plane sinking the enemy submarine in a report. A search plan was drafted.

7:15 A.M. U.S.S. Keosanqua (AT-38), a Navy tugboat, began to receive tow from Antares.

7:26 A.M. U.S.S. Helm (DD-388), a Bagley class destroyer, got underway from berth X-7 for departing buoys at West Loch. All hands were at their special sea detail stations.

Both boats were manned and in the water with instructions to follow the ship to west Loch. All magnetic compasses and chronometers (a precision time piece that has to be wound up) had been left in the U.S. Blue (DD-387) preparatory to departing.

7:43 A.M. local hostilities commenced with air raid on Pearl Harbor,

7:45 A.M. U.S.S. Avocet (AVP-4) Sea Plane Tender, was moored at Berth F- 1A, NAS Dock, Pearl Harbor. There were bomb explosions and planes were heard and sighted attacking Ford Island hangars.

U.S.S. Tucker (DD-374) nested alongside U.S.S. Whitney (AD-4) Destroyer Tender and the five-inch gun #3 could not be fired. All other guns and .50 caliber machine guns fired at attacking planes during all attacks. No loss of personnel or material. It is believed this vessel shot down three or four enemy planes.

There were two planes in hangar four and planes at the south end of hangar six with planes on the ramp. As soon as the raid started, three rifles were manned immediately. Two machine guns were manned in a plane being removed from the hangar. Machine gun position in planes were abandoned and the machine guns were moved to a safer position.

They set up two machine gun nests near south end of a hangar. Damage was received with seven planes burned, one wrecked and four damaged but able to be repaired. All hangar, office equipment, and stores were destroyed.

7:45 A.M. two planes moored in Kaneohe Bay. There were also two in the hangar and eight planes on the parking apron.

Upon being attacked, they manned machine guns in planes, mounted machine guns in pits and used rifles. They observed that the second wave of horizontal bombers did not release bombs. The losses included eight PBY-5's planes which were completely destroyed. Two planes were severely damaged and two were moderately damaged. All hangar, office equipment and stores destroyed.

7:50 A.M. U.S.S. Tracy (DD-214) moored port side to Berth 16, Navy Yard, Pearl Harbor and was under- going an overhaul.

U.S.S. Preble (DD-345) and U.S.S. Cummings (DD-365) moored to starboard in that order. The ships were totally disabled with main auxiliary machinery boilers and gun batteries dismantled.

7:50 A.M. U.S.S. Tautog (SS-199), a U.S. Navy submarine, observed enemies in a three-plane formation of dive bombers over Aiea fleet landing on southwest course. Enemy character was not discovered until bombs were dropped.

7:50 A.M. U.S.S. California (BB-44) sounded general quarters and set condition Zed (ZED condition is an order to close all watertight hatches and doors). Lieutenant Commander M. N. Little, First Lieutenant was The Officer of the Day who enforces the S.O.P. (Standard Operating Procedures) on board ship and prepared for getting underway.

7:50 A.M. U.S.S. Cassin (DD-372) Destroyer. Cassin's Commanding Officer observed about one hundred feet away from starboard side of dry dock #1 at an altitude of one hundred feet, there was an airplane with large red disks on bottom of wings. He sounded general quarters and made attempts to locate ammunition which were part of the 5" guns under overhaul. The .50 caliber machine guns were unlimbered (detached from holding unit).

7:50 A.M Patron 21's drafting of CPW2 search plan was completed.

7:50 A.M. or 7:53 A.M. the U.S.S. Oklahoma (BB-37) was struck by eight Japanese Type 91 Model2 torpedoes on port side. The ship listed which is a nautical term used when a ship takes on water. Meanwhile anti-aircraft batteries were manned and loaded and ready for action. General

Quarters were executed. The rapid listing of the ship and oil and water on the decks rendered service to guns ineffective.

7:50 A.M. U.S.S. Curtis (AV-4) a Sea Plane Tender was moored in berth X-22, condition X-RAY with number three boiler steaming. The ship was at General Quarters and was strafed by Japanese fighter planes.

A bomb was observed striking VP hangar at NAS which is a Patrol Squadron. Hangar Six is located at the south end of Ford Island in Pearl City, Hawaii.

U.S.S. Utah (BB-31/AG-18), U.S.S. Raleigh (CL-7), an Omaha class light cruiser and U.S.S. Richmond (CL-9), another Omaha class light cruiser, were attacked by torpedoes.

7:50 A.M. U.S.S. Pyro (AE-1), an ammunition ship was secured along West Loch dock. A noise of low-flying aircraft and explosion in Navy Yard area was heard. It was observed that two low wing monoplanes about one hundred feet above water was headed for U.S.S. Pyro (AE-1) ammunition ship. It was hit on port (left) beam. Planes zoomed clear of the ship and looked to be Japanese Zete or Zeros. General Quarters was again sounded, and preparations were made to get underway.

7:52 A.M. U.S.S. Avocet (AVP-4) Minesweeper sounded General Quarters and opened fire with 3" anti-aircraft battery. It hit a Japanese plane which had just turned away after torpedoing Battleship California. The plane burst into flames and crashed near Naval Hospital. There were 144 rounds of 3"/50 cal fired. Then there were 1750 rounds .30 cal. fired at 7:53 A.M.

U.S.S. Pruitt (DD-347) reported ten planes flying low at two hundred feet that bombed Ford Island and blew up the hangar.

7:53 A.M. U.S.S. Tern (AM-31) Minesweeper, notified authorities of an attack and made preparation for getting underway.

7:53 A.M. U.S.S. Tracy (DD-214) observed Battleship Row being attacked from astern by about ten Japanese dive bombers. Torpedo planes at about one hundred feet approached from the easterly direction attacking battleships.

The Officer of the Deck witnessed dive bombers attack Battleships (ten planes and Ford Island from North). The attack was followed by horizontal and dive bombers on same objective plus ships in dry dock. One dive bomber passed close enough to observe that it was a single engine by-plane probably type 94.

7:54 A.M. U.S.S. Gamble DD-123) Destroyer heard explosions on Ford Island.

7:55 A.M. U.S.S. Bagley (DD-386) moored at Navy Yard Pearl Harbor, berth B-22, for repairs to starboard bilge keel, sighted dive bombers in action over Hickam Field. They mistakenly were believed at that time to be U.S. Army bombers spotted on Radar.

Shortly after this time, an enemy plane approached from the direction of Merry Point at about 30-40 feet altitude and dropped torpedo on U.S.S Oklahoma (BB-37) and retired. The Oklahoma opened up with forward machine guns on attacking plane. Machine gun fire bagged the fifth Japanese plane. It swerved and a torpedo dropped and exploded in bank about thirty feet ahead of Bagley. The plane finally downed in the channel.

Action continued with the machine gunning of enemy planes. Three planes were believed to have been shot down by U.S.S. Bagley (DD-386) U.S.S. Bobolink (AM-20), a Lapwing class minesweeper, observed about twelve dive bombers centering their attack south hangars of Ford Island. U.S.S. Breese (DD-386), a Bagley class Destroyer was moored in berth D-3. Middle Loch, in nest with division order of ships from starboard U. S. S. Ramsay (DD-124) Destroyer, U.S.S. Breese (DD-122), a Wickes class Destroyer, U.S.S. Montgomery (DD-121) Destroyer, and U.S.S. Gamble (DD-123) observed bombing of the old hangar on Ford Island.

General Quarters was sounded with Set Condition "A", and preparations were made for getting under-way. Boats were sent boats to the landing to pick up men.

U.S.S. Cachalot (SS-170) a U.S. Navy Submarine, was moored at Berth # 1, Navy Yard, Pearl Harbor, undergoing a scheduled overhaul.

U.S.S. Castor (AKS-1), a General stores/supply ship, sounded General Quarters.

The ship berthed at Merry Point, the U.S.S. Conyngham (DD-371), a Destroyer, was heading north and moored starboard side to U.S.S. Whitney (AD-4,) a Destroyer, was at berth X-8.

U.S.S. Reid (DD-369), U.S.S. Tucker (DD-374), U.S.S. Case (DD-370), and U.S.S. Selfridge (DD-357), an outboard. Ship undergoing routine tender overhaul and receiving power from tender were all there. They noted a large fire on Ford Island and observed horizontal and dive-bombing planes attacking. General Quarters was sounded.

U.S.S Dewey (DD-349), a Farragut class Destroyer, observed U.S.S. Utah (BB—31/AG-16) to be torpedoed and to list rapidly.

U.S.S. Dewey (DD-349) at nest, Destroyer Division One, with U.S.S. Phelps (DD-360) moored alongside port side U.S.S. Dobbin (AD-3) a Destroyer Tender, at X-2 under overhaul.

7:55 A.M. U.S.S. Dolphin (SS-169), a U.S. Navy Submarine, was moored port side to Pier 4, Submarine Base, Pearl Harbor. Japanese aircraft delivered dive bomb and torpedo attack on Pearl Harbor. Sounded General Quarters.

U.S.S. Helm (DD-388) Destroyer, turned into West Loch channel and headed up toward deep water buoys.

U.S.S. Henley (DD-391) made an error in gangway watch in calling crew to quarters for muster at 7:55 A.M. General Alarm was sounded instead of Gas Alarm as was customary.

They observed the first torpedo plane attack on Utah. The crew proceeded to Battle Stations while General Alarm sounded the second time. Set material condition AFFIRM. They prepared for getting underway. They opened fire on a light bomber whose altitude was about 17,000 feet. The bomber was apparently steady on Northerly course, approaching from seaward and passing over Ford Island.

U.S.S. Honolulu (CL-48), a Brooklyn class light cruiser was moored port side to berth B21 Navy Yard Pearl with U.S.S. St. Louis (CL-49), a Brooklyn class Light cruiser, alongside starboard side.

Japanese Planes were seen diving on Hickam Field. At the same time, a wave of torpedo planes was seen approaching over fleet landing. Sounded General Quarters and passed word "Enemy Air Raid." The ship prepared to get underway. Anti-Aircraft batteries went into action gun by gun as they were manned. Fifty caliber and thirty caliber machine guns fired on enemy torpedo planes attacking the battleships.

From this time until raid ended, thirty caliber, fifty caliber and 5"/25 A.A. guns fired at every available target. Service ammunition expended 2,800 rounds of thirty caliber, 4,500 of fifty caliber and 250 rounds of 5"/25 caliber.

Twelve two-seat low wing monoplanes flying low from the southeast dropped one torpedo at each battleship. There were two planes destroyed. Eighteen low wing dive bombers from southeast bombed Hickam Field.

Minesweeper Division One was undergoing scheduled overhaul and moored in repair base. Guns and ammunition had been removed. The crew, except the watch on board, were living in Navy Yard receiving barracks.

7:55 A.M. Mine Division One saw Japanese planes attack the battleships. Men were sent to adjacent ships, U.S.S. New Orleans (CA-32) Heavy cruiser, U.S.S. San Francisco (CA-38) a Heavy cruiser, and U.S.S. Cummings (DD-44) Destroyer, to assist in manning Anti-Aircraft guns and handle ammunition.

Meanwhile receiving barracks sent our men to other ships to assist in fighting fires or handling ammunition. These men reported for duty to the battleship Pennsylvania (BB-38), Battleship California (BB-44), and U.S.S. Whitney (AD-4) a Dobbin class Destroyer.

Also, men were sent from the shipyard. All available Miner's Mates were sent to West Loch. Both .50 and .30 caliber Machine guns were reassembled and remounted, and ammunition was obtained from Navy ships, New Orleans, San Francisco, and U.S. Marine Corps Barracks. These guns were used against the enemy and helped with the later attacks. No ship of division suffered damage.

Patterson was moored at berth X-11, and battle stations were manned. They opened fire with main and fifty caliber batteries. The Patterson considered that at least one enemy plane was shot down. The enemy plane claimed by Patterson was one observed diving on Curtiss and was seen approaching from ahead at about four hundred feet altitude. The plane was seen to fall apart at the same time the shot was fired by #2 gun.

U.S.S. Phoenix (CL-46) light cruiser sighted the first Japanese attacking plane from Signal Bridge from north of Ford Island. The plane had all guns firing. It passed over stern of Raleigh and proceeded toward Ford Island Control Tower and dropped a bomb.

On December 7, the U.S.S. Preble (DD-345) was undergoing Navy Yard overhaul at berth Z-15 with no ammunition on board and the engineering plant dismantled.

The first attack on battleships began with about twenty torpedo planes. Planes were in low horizontal flight when observed and attacked from eastward. Enemy planes approached battleships to close range before releasing torpedoes. Raleigh Commanding Officer, Captain R.B. Simons, felt a dull explosion and looked out at the airport to see water boiling amid ships.

A report was received that Japanese were attacking fleet. Sounded General Quarters. Both ships planes were successfully hoisted out by hand power.

The Base Army Doctor was directed to report to U.S.S. Solace (AH-5) a U.S. Navy hospital ship. There were eleven damage repair parties sent to the capsized Utah with crew members trapped inside. The men had to be cut out of hull.

Navy Signalman sent a signal to send pontoon and a lighter alongside from Baltimore to Raleigh. These were delivered and secured to port quarter and acted as an out- rigger. Torpedoes, minus war heads, were pushed overboard and beached at Ford Island. All stanchions, boat skids and life rafts and booms were jettisoned. Both anchors let go.

The Officer of the Deck (O.O.D) on the U.S.S. Ramapo (AO-12), a Patoka class replenishment oiler, observed a Japanese dive bomber come in close and drop a couple of bombs. Sounded General Quarters and opened fire with Anti-Aircraft, Guns (3"/.23). Motor Torpedo Boats on board also opened fire with machine guns. Order of attack observed to be dive bombers strafing, torpedo planes, dive bombers bombing, horizontal planes bombing. Our personnel reported that a three-inch shell hit plane. No losses in personnel and no material damage.

Ramsay was moored at berth D-3 and observed a bomb land on the western end of Ford Island.

Reid observed an unidentified plane attacking Ford Island. U.S.S. Solace (AH-5), a Mercy class hospital ship, received a report of air raid, closed all watertight doors and ports, called away rescue parties while hospital facilities were prepared. They sent two motor launches with rescue parties to U.S.S. Arizona (BB-39).

U.S.S. Sumner (AG-32) was moored to the new dock at the southern end of the Submarine Base, port side to bow to eastward. Armament is four 3" 23 caliber Anti-Aircraft guns, four 50 caliber machine guns, and one 5" 51 caliber broadsides.

U.S.S. Swan (AM-34) a Minesweeper, Sounded General Quarters, in Marine Railway, boiler upkeep area. They observed a bomb dropped on South ramp of Fleet Air Base.

U.S.S. Tautog (SS-199), Navy submarine, observed about twenty Japanese planes approaching online of OAHU railroad tracks, and over Merry's point. Torpedoes were dropped from about fifty feet after submarine base pier was passed. The fourth plane in line and the plane near the end of line were shot down by this ship and U.S.S. Hulbert (DD-342) before torpedoes were dropped.

7:55 A.M. A Japanese plane flew from North to South over a fishpond adjacent to waterfront residence of Lt. R. B. Black, U. S. N. R. on the East shore of Pearl City Peninsula. A long burst of machine gun fire was directed at the breakwater enclosing the fishpond, and a single fisherman wearing a white shirt was seen to run rapidly along the breakwater. This material is forwarded to indicate that enemy pilots were directing fire at all individuals including civilians at a considerable distance from any military objectives.

7:56 A.M. U.S.S. Vestal (AR-4) Repair ship, sounded General Quarters. Manned A. A. Battery, 3" A. A. and .5" broadside and .30 cal. Machine gun.

U.S.S. Vireo (AM-52) Minesweeper moored inboard at Coal Dock (seaward end) with U.S.S. Turkey (AM-13) Minesweeper, U.S.S. Bobolink (AM-20) Minesweeper, and U.S.S. Rail (AM-26) Minesweeper, outboard. U.S.S. WIDGEON (AM-22) Minesweeper had no remarks except machine gun and rifle fire used against enemy. They had no losses or damage.

U.S.S. West Virginia (BB-48) Battleship, passed word, "Away fire and rescue party" followed by General Quarters. Two heavy shocks felt on the hull of West Virginia apparently forward and on port side. The ship began to list rapidly to port. Another third heavy shock felt to port. A plane on top of turret 4 caught on fire. A heavy explosion occurred with about 20-degree list on ship to port. Central station directed to counter-flood. Damage control teams actively worked on flooding.

The following last explosion flashed a flame about fifteen feet high occurred forward on Arizona. A second flash occurred on the Arizona higher than the fore- top. Burning debris rained on Quarter Deck of West Virginia.

After the two Arizona explosions at 8:10 A.M. Arizona was struck by a 1,760-pound armer piercing bomb which hit her main ammunition magazine holding 1,000,000 pounds of ammunition. The projectile impact caused ammunition and fuels to ignite causing a massive explosion literally causing the battleship to lift out of the water. As she sank, she was hit with a second bomb near her Quarterdeck.

The West Virginia began to right itself when a large fire broke out at midships. Word was received from central station to abandon ship. A wall of flame was advancing toward the West Virginia and Tennessee from the Arizona.

The ship's personnel on the West Virginia began to abandon ship as the fire had grown out of control.

Meanwhile, magazines of West Virginia had been flooded. West Virginia personnel reported to U.S.S. Tennessee that remaining survivors were ashore and elsewhere. Others were sent back to West Virginia to fight fires. All fires were finally extinguished on Monday, December 8th at 7:56 A.M.

Bobolink was on Ready duty status and moored at next end of coal docks with Vireo and Turkey inboard and Rail outboard. They were informed by gangway watch that Japanese planes were bombing us. Sounded General Quarters.

The U.S.S. Gamble saw a wave of about fifty Japanese planes attacked battleships on Battleship Row located near Ford Island and Naval Air Station, at Hickman Field. At Ford Island, planes were flying at low altitudes about five hundred feet over battleships from the direction of Diamond Head, about seven hundred feet over Ford Island.

Five successive waves of the attack of about ten planes each were accomplished. Minesweeper Division Two went to General Quarters and set Condition "A".

U.S.S. Thornton (DD-270) reports attack by Japanese Aircraft commenced, General Alarm was sounded, and all hands went to Air Defense Stations. Thornton moored port side to dock at Berth S-1, Submarine Base Pearl Harbor. Stations manned were as follows: Control, Machine Gun Battery Control, Repair, and 4 .50 cal. Machine Guns, three .30 Cal. Lewis Machine Guns, three .30 Browning automatic rifles, and twelve .30 cal. Springfield rifles.

7:57 A.M. Ensign Chiles of U.S.S. Jarvis (DD-393) called Lieutenant Ford and said, "Someone is bombing us."

U.S.S. Breese (DD-122) opened fire with .50 cal. machine guns.

Conyngham observed torpedo planes attacking Raleigh, Utah and Detroit from the west.

U.S.S. Dewey (DD-349) sounded General Quarters.

U.S.S. Helena (CL-50) Light cruiser was moored at 1010 Dock, Berth 2, port side to Dock.

U.S.S. Oglala (CM-4) Mine layer, was alongside starboard side and reported observing planes over Ford Island, 14,000 ft. altitude.

Signalman on bridge with previous duty on Asiatic Station identified planes immediately. General Alarm sounded and service ammunition broke out.

U.S.S. Hull (DD-350) at General Quarters, prepared to get underway.

7:57 A.M. New Orleans was moored at Berth 16, Navy Yard, Pearl Harbor undergoing Engine Repairs, receiving power and light from the Dock. Enemy planes were sighted dive-bombing Ford Island. General Quarters was sounded.

7:57 A.M. the Pennsylvania was In Dry Dock #1. Three Propeller Shafts were removed.

Destroyers Cassin and Downes were in the Dock ahead of Pennsylvania. The Floating Dock West of new dry dock adjoining Pennsylvania was occupied by Shaw. Cruiser Helena and Oglala were at Berth B-2 which was Pennsylvania's normal berth.

California was in F-3 and Maryland in F-4 inboard. Oklahoma was outboard, Berth F-6, Tennessee inboard, West Virginia outboard, F7 Arizona, F8 Nevada.

Machine Guns were in foremast manned and condition watch of Anti-Aircraft personnel available. Ship received steam, water, and power from shipyard.

Explosions were heard on end of Ford Island, and they realized an Air Raid was in progress after the second explosion. Air defense sounded, followed by General Quarters. Set Condition YOKE (YOKE is set at sea, when entering or leaving port).

7:57 A.M. U.S.S. Sumner (AGS-5) Submarine Tender, signal watch and Quartermaster on Bridge sighted ten Japanese dive bombers attacking the Navy Yard. They observed two explosions in the Navy Yard and sounded the alarm.

7:57 A.M. U.S.S. Trever (DD-339) Minesweeper Division Four was moored at Buoys D-7, bow toward Pearl City. In order from the North were the Trever, Wasmuth (DD-338), Zane (DD-337), and Perry (DD-340).

General Quarters was sounded at the time the first bomb was dropped by Japanese on North side of Ford Island.

7:57 A.M. Wasmuth reported first Japanese planes attacked. It went to General Quarters at once with all guns in action within three minutes. However, as the ship was inside a nest of four ships, only two after guns could bear. They made all preparations for getting underway.

7:57 A.M. Patron 21 was the first bomb dropped near VP-22 Hangar. Message order was broadcast to all ships present "AIR RAID P. H. X. THIS IS NOT DRILL." A similar message was sent by Cincpac Zane moored bow and stern to nest with Mine Division Four at buoys D-7, The order was from port to starboard for Trever, Wasmuth, Zane and Perry.

First call to standby colors sounded which is the raising of the American Flag. Signalmen on watch observed a single Japanese plane drop a bomb from about 10,000 feet on the southern end of Ford Island after approach from Northward.

Sounded General Quarters and manned Anti-Aircraft battery and commenced firing with A. A. battery at all Japanese planes passing within reasonable distances. All preparations were made to get underway.

7:58 A.M. U.S.S. Antares (AG-10) Cargo ship heard an explosion in Pearl Harbor and observed Japanese planes delivering attack.

7:58 A.M. U.S.S Bagley (DD-386) observed a torpedo plane come in from the direction of Merry Point between Navy Yard and Kuahua Island at an altitude of thirty or forty feet. It was headed for the Oklahoma. About two or three hundred yards from the Oklahoma, the plane dropped its torpedo and hit the Oklahoma at midship. General Quarters was sounded, and firing commenced. The fourth plane to fire upon the Oklahoma was seen to crash in channel off Officers' Club landing. The machine gun fire on the eighth plane made it swerve to left causing torpedo to drop and explode in bank about thirty feet ahead of Bagley.

Number one machine gun downed the plane in Navy Yard channel. The third torpedo plane hit by Bagley was observed headed for light cruisers Honolulu and St. Louis astern of Bagley. It went out of control, dropped its torpedo, and seemed to hit L-head Crane in Navy Yard. This was about the eleventh plane to come in.

The next plane hit by Bagley came in over the dock but was downed with a short burst. A torpedo dropped in lumber pile, and it was believed that a plane crashed on dock.

Th fifth plane brought down by Bagley came down on starboard side, nose directly up into air and spun into a crash losing its torpedo.

The sixth plane brought down by Bagley was a dive bomber during the second phase of attack and after the torpedo attack. This plane was shot down by five-inch guns and those from other ships.

7:58 A.M. U.S.S. Cummings (DD-365) observed enemy planes making a torpedo attack on battleships moored to East side of Ford Island. Sounded General Quarters.

7:58 A.M. Gamble went to General Quarters and opened fire with .50 cal. machine guns on planes passing over nest at about eight hundred feet altitude. Set Material Condition Affirm except for certain protected Ammunition Passages.

Jarvis General Quarters sounded along with Hulbert.

A torpedo plane was sighted heading West over East Lock preparing to launch a torpedo against a battleship off Ford Island. Hulbert reports bringing down one Japanese torpedo plane by .50 cal. A. A. fire from Berth S-3, Submarine Base.

7:58 A.M. U.S. S. Hull (DD-350) Gangway watch opened fire with .45 caliber pistol on two planes crossing bow within fifty yards.

7:58 A.M. Mugford moored port side to the U. S. S. Sacramento (PG-19) Gun Boat, Berth No. 6, Navy Yard.

U. S. S. Jarvis moored port side to Mugford when the attack started. Japanese planes were diving on Ford Island. Several large bombs struck the sea plane landing ramp followed by explosions near hangars. Several Japanese planes came in low from Southwest and released torpedoes which struck Oklahoma and West Virginia. Enemy torpedo planes came in continuously from same direction and fired torpedoes at the Battleships.

7:58 A.M. Tennessee was attacked by enemy planes (Japanese). Oily water around stern was burning. Canvas awning on stern were on fire, Turret III. Smoke was pouring into Repair Locker. Smoke was so thick that you could not see. Damage Control Repair team reported that they had men on standby to respond to magazine flood, Turret III. All boats on fire. Fire in Main deck, secondary aft. Fire in maintop seems to be out. West Virginia's quarterdeck and her planes on fire. Fire on Turret III. The crew was unable to get much needed morphine out of doctor's room because it was unsafe. Men reported that the room was too hot to go in and cut the safe open.

Squadron of planes diving on Navy Yard. Repair I, unit 3, had to abandon station because it was too hot. Fire on topside seemed to be under control. D-310 A was all right. Set Condition ZED (ZED is a condition where all watertight hatches and doors are secured) in lower handling room of Turret III.

The Oklahoma seems to be capsizing.

The California is down by the stern.

The West Virginia has pretty bad fire below Signal Bridge.

Tennessee was hit twice, soon after attack began. One bomb hit on face of Turret II, and bomb hit on top of Turret III, penetrating.

7:58 A.M. U.S.S. Thornton (DD-270) commenced firing with .50 cal. machine gun battery followed immediately by .30 cal. machine guns and .30 cal. rifles.

7:59 A.M. U.S.S. Reid (DD-369) went to General Quarters.

Rigel witnessed a Ford Island attack by ten dive bombers from North at ten thousand feet.

7:59 A.M. Gamble opened fire with 3"/23 cal. AA guns, firing as planes came within range, fuses set 3 to 8 secs.

7:59 A.M. U.S.S. Helm (DD-388) sighted an enemy plane in shallow dive over Ford Island, headed Northwest. It was observed that the first bomb hit on hangar at southwest end of Ford Island. The crew was called to General Quarters. Opened magazines and got ammunition to guns.

Jarvis Lieutenant Ford and Lieutenant Johnson of Jarvis reach the bridge. Japanese torpedo planes were coming in at thirty to sixty second intervals, approaching from Merry Point direction and attacking Battleships.

7:59 A.M. Sumner observed torpedo planes approach over Southeast Loch attacking Battleships, circling Ford Island, and flying off to southwest.

Whitney observed an air raid attack by Japanese Army Air Force and explosions on Ford Island. Whitney moored bow and stern to buoys X-8 and X-8x, six fathoms of water, supplying steam, electricity, fresh and flush- water to Connyngham, Reid, Tucker, Case, and Selfridge, moored alongside to port.

7:59 A.M. U.S.S. Pelias (AS-14) Submarine Tender, reports nine dive bombers attacked out of direction of sun the battleships. One broke off and dive-bombed Pennsylvania.

8:00 A.M. two officers from a ship were hiking in back of Aiea, located near the city of Honolulu, Hawaii, and they witnessed the attack. They stated later that three separate flights of planes appeared at three levels: low, medium, and high from the north.

8:00 A.M. Vireo Commanding Officer heard an explosion. Immediately, Japanese planes were seen, and General Quarters sounded.

8:00 A.M. Antares was under machine gun fire. The topside was hit by machine gun bullets, bomb, and shell fragments. Being unarmed, no offensive tactics were possible. In order to avoid placing ship and personnel in jeopardy, authority was requested to enter Honolulu Harbor.

8:00 A.M. COMINBATFOR Comicraft on U.S.S. Oglala (CM-4) Minelayer ship, observed an enemy bomb fall seaward and Ford Island, but there was no damage. The next bomb caused fires near waters. Flames flared up from structures at the south end of island.

The next bomb fell alongside or on board seven battleships moored at F-1 east side of Ford Island. Japanese planes flew between fifty and one hundred feet of water, dropping three torpedoes or mines in channel online between Oglala and seaward end of Ford Island.

Twenty torpedoes hit Oglala and Helena simultaneously. These ships were moored abreast of B-2 of ten dock Oglala outboard. Both ships opened fire with A. A. battery. Oglala signaled C-C possibility that mines had been dropped. Two contract tugs were hailed to haul Oglala aft of Helena. Submersible pumps for Oglala were obtained from Helena but could not be used as no power was available.

It was observed that one Japanese plane was shot down. Planes were strafing (using machine guns) as well as bombing. There were four battleships hit with bombs, fires broke out, and one battleship, the U.S.S. Utah, turned over. Enemy planes appeared to fly in groups of six to ten planes.

8:00 A.M. VP-21 CPW2 search plan was transmitted by radio and telephone. There was difficulty experienced in communicating with Kanehoe.

8:00 A.M. Cassin saw another plane come down to about seventy-five feet on parallel course drydock #1. The plane dropped a torpedo aimed at California at range two hundred yards. U.S.S. Castor had 3" A. A. and 30 cal. machine guns and commenced firing against enemy torpedo planes, low and close aboard, and against dive bombers. One enemy torpedo plane was observed at about five hundred to seven hundred yards range and five hundred feet altitude due aft of the ship and heading across to Ford Island with parts of fuselage shot away. The plane grounded either on Ford Island or beyond. A covered lighter was removed alongside with 450 serial depth charges.

8:00 A.M. Dolphin, a U.S. Navy submarine with machine guns and rifles manned fired at enemy aircraft which were flying very low. Ready identification could be made by the large red balls on each wing. A report was received that a plane had been shot down and dove into channel off pier 5.

8:00A.M. Utah was torpedoed. General alarm was sounded, and word passed throughout the ship to man battle stations and prepare to get underway immediately. Rigel was in the vicinity of #1 dry dock. Ten/ten dock was strafed and bombed by thirteen dive bombers from the south at an altitude of six hundred to one hundred feet.

Whitney sounded general quarters. The first plane passed over the ship at a low altitude, strafing Helm. There were torpedo planes sighted approaching from the direction of Barber's Point. They passed over West Loch channel and dropped torpedoes either in North Channel or across the Island. Targets for these planes appeared to be ships in berths F-9 to F-13. The planes came in low, and several strafed the ship. All bullets missed the ship by a few feet. No fire was opened, since the forward machine guns, which could bear were covered with preservative grease and had to be cleaned before they could fire.

Helm backed engines and commenced maneuvering the ship out of West Loch channel to head for entrance.

8:00 A.M. Jarvis Ensign Greene, Officer of the Deck of Jarvis, reported on bridge. Prior to this, he had been directing activities around the quarterdeck. He was told to go to there after firing battery.

Ensign Chiles was actively organizing the forward battery without orders. Ensign Fleece was already on the director. Orders were given to open fire and Mugford commenced assembly of engineering plant which had been placed out of commission for yard overhaul. They connected the fuel oil hose to yard line. 8,000 gallons total on board.

8:00 A.M. U.S.S. Phoenix (CL-46) witnessed the bombing attack on the battleships. The markings on the enemy planes varied from swastikas and rising sun painted on the fuselage.

Raleigh opened fire with AA battery of 3"/50 cal. 1.1" and .50 cal. guns. The ship started to list to port and received a report that a torpedo had struck #2 fireroom. #1 and 2 firerooms and forward engine-room were completely flooded. The fire in #3 went out which directed counter-flooding. As it appeared that ship would capsize, orders were given to jettison top- side.

8:00 A.M. Raleigh had both planes successfully hoisted out by hand. The doctor was directed to report to Solace. A damage repair party was sent to capsized Utah to cut men out of hull. A signal was sent to send pontoons and lighter from alongside Baltimore to Raleigh. These were delivered and secured to port quarter and acted as outrigger. Torpedoes minus war- heads were beached at Ford Island. All stanchions, boat skids, and life rafts and booms were jettisoned. Anchors were let go.

8:01 A.M. the Utah was attacked by a torpedo plane and bombing plane. Sounded General Quarters. The ship received severe underwater hit on frame 84, port side. This was followed by another hit which caused the ship to list fifteen degrees. Passed word "all hands on deck."

It was not possible to repel the attack as all ammunition was in magazines and secured. 5" and 1.1 guns were covered with steel housing.

The .50 and .30 caliber machine guns were dismounted and stowed below decks. The ship was covered with two layers of six by twelve timbers.

The above conditions necessitated because the Utah was being used by ships as a bombing target during current operations. A bomb explosion was received in port forecastle.

8:01 A.M. Pruitt reported that the Oklahoma and the Arizona had been attacked from a southerly direction. A number of torpedo planes had attacked from southeast.

Nevada observed the enemy air attack. Sounded general quarters. Two machine guns forward and two aft had been already on continuous watch under the alert program.

Mugford sounded General Quarters.

8:01 A.M. Sumner saw dense smoke rising behind Kuahuai Peninsula and it was believed to be from the Arizona. There was blazing oil floating down from the line of battleships. #3 gun was manned and opened fire four minutes after the attack on Navy Yard was observed, and before any other gun in the vicinity had commenced firing. They made a direct hit on and destroyed a torpedo plane which was making its approach on the battleships.

8:01 A.M. Helena opened fire and was hit by torpedo from a range five hundred yards, starboard side, approximately on frame seventy-five, eighteen feet below water line. Four near misses from bombs were received and one strafing attack was survived with little damage. Gas masks and protective clothing was issued.

Once the gun opposition was in full swing, Japanese planes were noted to turn away from gunfire or keep at respectable altitude.

8:02 A.M. Dewey crew manned four .50 caliber machine guns and fired at planes attacking battle ships and Ford Island.

Trever opened fire with .50 caliber machine guns.

Nevada opened fire with machine guns on enemy planes approaching on port beam. One plane was brought down one hundred yards off Nevada's port quarter. One plane dropped a torpedo which struck the Nevada on port bow.

8:02 A.M. Pennsylvania was attacked by about twelve to fifteen torpedo planes from west and south; They reported as first ship opened fire on plane. After release of torpedoes, three enemy planes came in low from port beam strafing Pennsylvania, though it was not affected. The bearing of the torpedo attack and the one enemy plane was observed bursting into flames about two thousand yards on starboard bow.

There were dive bombing attacks and torpedo attacks on Pearl Harbor, and dive bombing attacks on Hickam Field.

8:03 A.M. Cummings opened fire on the Japanese torpedo planes. Then the California opened fire with machine guns and ready guns on the torpedo planes. Swan opened fire with 3" A. A. guns. All sea valves and hatches closed and commenced placing boilers in commission. One direct hit was observed with 3" gun and the plane crashed beyond the drydock area. No material damage suffered.

Cachalot had enemy planes pass within range and with an arc of guns. They opened up with .30 and .50 caliber machine guns.

8:03 A.M. Nevada opened fire with 5" A. A. Members of the crew claim both broadsides scored direct hits on torpedo plane which disintegrated in midair.

8:04 A.M. Jarvis machine guns opened fire. Whitney commenced firing with .50 cal. AA guns. They received the signal to get underway.

8:05 A.M. Mugford opened fire with 50 caliber MGs. They shot down a Japanese plane at an altitude of eight hundred on the starboard quarter, passing aft on starboard hand. This plane had fired a torpedo at the U.S.S. Oglala.

8:05A.M. New Orleans sighted enemy torpedo planes on port quarter, flying low across stern. Rifle fire and pistol fire opened from fantail as the first planes flew by to launch torpedoes at battleships. Manned 1.1 battery and machine guns aft in time to fire at three or four enemy planes.

8:06 A.M. Tracy observed torpedo planes coming in from an easterly direction and launching torpedoes at battleships at Ford Island. At first attack, the ship closed up as much as possible and broke out fighting equipment.

8:05 A.M. Vestal opened fire and shortly after A. A. breach jammed blast from Arizona cleared gun station, killing one man. They fired with machine guns on enemy planes until they were withdrawn. They fired at a torpedo plane which was seen to burst into flame and disappear over Ford Island.

The following personnel damage was done: nine dead, seven missing, nineteen in hospital.

8:05 A.M. U.S.S. Rigel (AD-13) a Destroyer Tender was attacked from an altitude of 125 feet from southeast by twelve torpedo planes at three to five hundred yard range.

Helm opened fire with after machine guns at planes over the main channel, followed shortly by forward machine guns firing at passing torpedo planes.

Hull #4 machine gun opened fire.

Curtiss was firing with 5" local control and .50 caliber machine guns. They lighted off boilers 1, 2 and 4.

8:05 A.M. Utah Listed about forty feet to port. Attacking planes strafed the crew as the ship was abandoned.

Sumner had a torpedo plane pass close aboard within one hundred yards of the ship's stern on west course at an altitude of seventy-five feet. It leveled off for launching a torpedo at battleship row. It was struck by a direct hit from Sumner's #3 A. A. gun, range three hundred yards. The plane disintegrated in smoke and sank in fragments. The torpedo believed to have sunk without exploding.

Jarvis 5" opened fire. #3 gun was believed to be the first 5" gun in the harbor to open fire.

Breese opened fire with 3" A. A. Guns.

8:05 A.M. Ramsay sounded general quarters and opened fire with .50 cal. and 3" guns. The Ramsay liberty party was returning in the Montgomery boat and was strafed by torpedo planes which were observed to fire three torpedoes into Utah and Raleigh.

8:05 A.M. Gamble mounted and commenced firing with .30 cal. machine guns on galley deck house. U.S.S. Blue (DD-387) opened fire with .50 caliber machine guns on Japanese planes that were diving on ships in the harbor. Cassin observed Helena open fire followed by Pennsylvania.

8:05 A.M. California reported two torpedoes struck port side, frame 100, making a forty foot long hole extending from first seam below armor belt to bilge keel.

8:06 A.M. Vestal was struck by two bombs. Vestal moored to port side of Arizona Berth-F7. One bomb struck starboard side frame 44 and penetrated three decks, exploding in GSK Stores which held all the ship's dry good supplies. This explosion also cut the fire main and electric cables in crew space. The hold set on fire and was wrecked. Another bomb struck at frame-110 on port side, passed through the ships and fuel oil tank. A bomb explosion forward damaged practically all stores. The heat of the explosion necessitated flooding fwd magazines. The material damaged consisted of three life rafts, six mooring lines, one gangway, port lenses and windows broken.

8:06 A.M. Phoenix made radio signal to ships of sector four "prepare to get underway".

Pruitt observed a Japanese bomber shot down. Arizona listed sharply with smoke and flames. Bobolink and Turkey commenced firing. The other boats in nest were directed to tie up to destroyer buoys adjacent to battle rafts in order to disperse.

8:07 A.M. Blue opened fire with 5"/38 caliber guns on Japanese planes. The engine room was ordered immediately to light off No. 2 boiler (#1 was already steaming) and made all preparations for getting underway. The repair party cleared the ship for action and made all preparations for slipping quickly from the mooring.

8:07 A.M. Helm opened fire with 5" battery. No hits were observed.

Hull #1 5"/38 cal. opened fire.

8:07 A.M. The Phoenix had one plane burning in water at end of pipe-line astern of berth F-8.

8:08 A.M. Curtiss sent Engine Room Emergency Underway signal.

8:08 A.M. Cummings opened fire on horizontal bombers approaching over Navy Yard from southerly direction.

8:08 A.M. Conyngham opened fire with 5" gun and machine guns on attacking planes.

8:08 A.M. U.S.S. Mugford (DD-3890) witnessed and filmed the U. S. S. Oklahoma capsizing by crew member who normally let the Y.M.C.A. borrow it on Sundays. Battleship West Virginia listed heavily to port side.

8:10 A.M. Arizona blew up. Whitney was preparing for getting underway. Supplies issued to destroyers alongside.

HULL #5 gun, 5"/38 cal. opened fire, followed by guns #2, #3, and #4.

8:10 A.M. Thornton's first dive bombing attack ended.

8:10 A.M. Cummings commenced preparation for getting underway in accordance with the general signal. They opened fire main battery on dive bombers over battleships.

8:10 A.M. Enemy aircraft bomb struck hangar and aircraft parking space adjacent to VP-24 parking area. One plane suffered a severed wing. A U.S. plane was then machine gunned and caught fire. The fire was extinguished, and plane was repaired and ready for service. The plane that was undergoing structural changes was not damaged and is now operating. Personnel present mounted machine guns in available planes and opened fire on attacking planes. One low-winged biplane flying from across hangar 54 on course about 250 lost both wings.

New Orleans utilized all batteries except eight inch battery in action. The area around berths 14-19 inclusive were subjected to dive bombing attacks by approximately ten enemy planes. The attack was turned away by combined fire of Honolulu and New Orleans.

Three bombs were observed dropping. One fell ahead of, and another fell astern of the Rigel. These failed to explode. A third bomb landed midway between Rigel and New Orleans exploding and causing damage from flying fragments.

During the raid, yard power failed or was cut off leaving vessels in darkness without power except auxiliary battery power. There was a heavy drain of machinery raising steam from getting underway and so much exhausted auxiliary batteries that lighting was very dim and of practically no use. All work in engineering spaces, magazines and ammunition passageways had to be conducted by flashlight. Hoists and guns were worked by hand with consequent reduction of volume of fire. Anti-Aircraft directors were off ship.

8:10 A.M. Utah Listed 80 to port mooring lines parting and two minutes later the ship capsized and was abandoned. Salvage operations undertaken immediately in order to rescue the entrapped personnel. There were thirty-two men rescued. Estimated number of torpedoes to hit ship was about five. No bombs were observed to have hit.

8:10 A.M. Phoenix machine gun battery opened fire on attacking planes.

8:10 A.M. Dewey guns 1-2-3 and 5 5" had no power on the ship.

8:10 A.M. Helm fired from port and the machine gun hit the plane approaching from South. The plane veered sharply, caught on fire, and crashed behind trees near Hickam Field. Damage to enemy was one plane shot down by machine gun fire.

8:10 A.M. Cassin observed Japanese plane crash over tree near hospital. Five at high altitude of 12,000 ft. Bombers passed overhead from forward aft and dropped large bombs.

8:10 A.M. Pruitt Observed Oklahoma roll over.

8:10 A.M. Gamble commenced preparing to get underway. Lighted off four boilers.

8:10 A.M. California opened fire with 5" guns on dive bombers. West Virginia's Commanding Officer, Captain M. S. Bennion, was mortally wounded. Whitney set condition affirm. Commenced firing with 3" A. A. guns.

8:10 A.M. Jarvis counted six or seven torpedoes in Oklahoma, Nevada, West Virginia, and Arizona. Apparently, Arizona's forwarded magazine exploded. It was noted that Oglala was torpedoed alongside Helena at 10/10 dock.

8:10 A.M. Reid opened fire with after machine guns.

8:10 A.M. Whitney had no material or personnel damage.

8:10 A.M. Pelias reports formation of high altitude planes came in from southwest attacking battleships and Ford Island followed by another wave from the same direction. Torpedo planes were small and carried only one bomb. Dive bombers also small and carried but one bomb.

8:10 A.M. Rail was at coal docks nested with four mine sweeps. Opened fire with 3" A. A. fifteen minutes after first bomb dropped on Pearl Harbor. Opened fire with .30 machine guns, rifles, and pistols twenty minutes after first attack.

A string of twenty bombs fell in channel astern. Shrapnel fell throughout ship. No material or personnel damage.

8:12 A.M. Mugford and Oglala were listing to port. The attack started again with heavy anti-aircraft fire.

8:12 A.M. Outgoing hostilities with Japan commenced with air raid on Pearl Harbor.

8:12 A.M. COMSECTOR FOUR: Sector 4 Prepare to get underway.

8:12 A.M. Hull had all machine guns plus two automatic rifles on the bridge and one on after deck and all were firing.

8:12 A.M. Rigel had torpedo planes attacking from Southeast at five hundred feet and attacked Battleships from an altitude of one hundred twenty-five and a range from three hundred to five hundred yards.

8:12 A.M. Task Force 8 received message from Combat Information Center (CIC) about the Air Raid on Pearl Harbor. This is no drill.

This time about coincided with expected arrival of the U.S.S. Enterprise (CV-6) a Yorktown class, aircraft carrier plane at Pearl Harbor.

The Task Force Commander was first concerned that planes were assumed to be unfriendly by Pearl Harbor defenses. It was not until subsequent dispatches were received that it was realized that hostilities with Japan had begun.

TF-8 operated in area South Kaula Rock for air attack should an enemy be located North or South of Oahu. No authentic information is available regarding location. They maintained combat and inner air patrols.

8:12 A.M. U.S.S. Sicard (DD-346) was undergoing overhaul in Navy Yard starboard side to Pruitt Berth 18. The ship was totally disabled as to main and auxiliary machinery and gun battery. They observed a squadron of Japanese planes coming in from Southwest, diving from 5,000 feet on Ford Island.

8:13 A.M. Conyngham observed an attacking plane being shot down by fire from the nest. The plane crashed near Curtiss.

8:13 A.M. Helm passed gate vessel.

8:15 A.M. Aircraft in flight informed hostilities with Japan commenced with air raid on Pearl Harbor. VP-21 was directed to search sector 240-280 for carriers. Ten miles south of Barbers Point, plane 24VP-4 sighted unidentified submarine near force consisting of U.S.S. Indianapolis (CA-35), a Portland class heavy cruiser, and four destroyers. The submarine made a crash dive, and the spot was marked by float lights. They completed the search through two hundred miles and returned to Pearl Harbor.

8:15 A.M. Battleship Pennsylvania reports that Nevada is underway and about on Pennsylvania's starboard quarter. This was a distance of about six hundred yards when dive bombing attack was observed approaching the Pennsylvania on port bow. There are ten or fifteen planes coming in succession just before reaching Pennsylvania. About two-thirds of the planes appear to swerve to the left. A number of them dropping bombs at the Nevada with one dive bomber dropping a bomb on Shaw in floating dry dock and set it on fire.

Nevada observed to slowly swing around head to port broadside to channel, on fire forward.

8:15 A.M. Vireo observed 2nd Group of enemy planes fly toward Hickam Field. Vireo opened fire expending twenty-two rounds 3" A. A. ammunition.

8:15 A.M. Riggel undergoing major repairs and conversion at Navy yard. No motive power available. All power except from yard. Air attack began. As this vessel had no armament, no offensive action could be taken. Accordingly, rescue work was commenced on West Virginia personnel. About one hundred men (in track of burning oil) had been blown into the water. These were rescued first.

The torpedo bombing and machine gun, a total of thirty-four assaults on the West Virginia, continued while the rescue operations progressed. One rescue boat was struck by a bomb and sunk. The crew was thrown into water. The West Virginia was moored B-13 Navy yard with major repairs necessary and services from Navy yard.

8:15 A.M. Sicard set condition of readiness "AFFIRM." Two2 fire parties were formed fore and aft.

8:15 A.M. Mugford shot down one enemy plane bearing astern making approach on battleship at altitude of twenty feet off water. The plane crashed on Ford Island aflame, and the torpedo was not launched.

8:15 A.M. Phoenix A. A. Battery opened fire.

8:15 A.M. Cassin observed another group of six high altitude bombers passed over-head and let loose bombs.

8:15 A.M. Pruitt observed twelve bombing planes in close "V" formation bombed (horizontal attack) from ten thousand feet from Southwest.

8:15 A.M. Jarvis had all guns and machine guns in action. Mugford noted to be delivering high volume of fire. **8:15 A.M.** Sumner checked fire.

8:17 A.M. Cincpac directed Combat wing to locate enemy force.

8:17 A.M. Helm sighted conning tower of submarine to right of channel, North- ward of buoy #1. Gave orders to open fire, pointer fire, but submarine submerged before guns could get on.

8:18 A.M. Conynhan opened fire with remaining 5" guns at horizontal bombers passing overhead in direction of Schofield Barracks.

8:20 A.M. Tracy sent men to Cummings to assist Anti-Aircraft batteries and approximate fifteen men to Pennsylvania to fight fires.

8:20 A.M. Helm opened fire on submarine off Tripod Reef, no hits observed. Submarine appeared to be touching bottom on ledge of reef, and in line of breakers. Steering motor short-circuited and the bridge lost steering control.

8:20 A.M. Sicard was manned with two .30 cal. machine guns. Bombers began to attack ships at 10/10 dock and battleships in vicinity of Ford Island. Sicard hits were observed on planes, but no apparent damage was done.

8:20 A.M. Vestal observed a torpedo pass astern and hit Arizona. Simultaneously Arizona received bomb hit followed by her forward magazine exploding. Latter started fires aft and amidship of Vestal. Shortly after that, Arizona observed to be settling and fuel oil between Vestal and Arizona ignited.

8:20 A.M. Pyro opened fire on planes.

8:20 A.M. Mugford opened fire with 5"/38 battery.

8:20 A.M. Sumner ship ready for getting underway. Members of broadside gun crew and available engineers were armed with rifles and BAR's and stationed in upper works to act as snipers.

8:20 A.M. California torpedo struck port side, frame 47, making an irregular hole 27 x 32 ft., the top of which is six feet below bottom of armor belt.

8:20 A.M. Solace reports boat loads of casualties began to arrive. By this time all hospital supplies and facilities had been prepared for maximum service.

8:20 A.M. Nevada attack slackened.

8:20 A.M. Reid opened fire with after 5"/38 caliber on high altitude and dive bombers.

8:20 A.M. 0820 Whitney observed Japanese plane fall in flames north channel vicinity X-5.

8:20 A.M. Cummings hull in air attack; ceased firing. Lack of D/C power prevented use of director. Sound powered telephones and local control used.

8:20 A.M. Hulbert claims share in bringing down a bomber.

8:20 A.M. Helm fired at enemy plane with forward machine guns. Nevada received heavy bombing attack.

8:21 A.M. Helm observed torpedo pass close under stern on a northerly course.

8:25 A.M. Tracy ready to open fire with 3 .30 caliber.

8:25 A.M. Mugford signal received that parachutists or wrecked pilot were landing in Hickam Field.

8:25 A.M. California opened fire on horizontal bombers at ten thousand feet with 5" guns.

8:25 A.M. Breese received signal to get underway but being inside nest could not do so.

8:25 A.M. Outgoing To COMTASKGR 12 and COMTASKGR 8: Report position.

8:25 A.M. Sumner opened fire on ten dive bombers attacking Navy Yard Dry Dock. These planes approached from cloud bank in Southeast. Heard terrific explosion in Navy Yard-vicinity of Dry Dock followed by dense cloud of smoke. Dive bomber passed three hundred yards from Sumner and Destroyer's Hulbert and Thornton with the tail of plane ignited. Plane turned southward and disappeared over Halawa district. Observed six horizontal bombers approaching from southeast at eight thousand feet. Japanese planes circled and approached Ford Island from Southwest and dropped bombs over Dry Docks. Planes then circled to Southeast. One plane left its formation, turned towards Navy Yard losing altitude rapidly, passed Sumner at four hundred feet altitude at a range six hundred yards It was fired on by Sumner. When over center Southeast Loch, the plane began smoking and was lost in thick smoke over Navy Yard. It was a two-seater monoplane, gunner in rear seat protected by shield, orange disc on side just abaft rear cockpit.

8:25 A.M. Curtiss attacked by bombers.

8:26 A.M. Planes crossing low ahead of nest to Northeast were taken under fire by Conyngham and nest. One burst into flames and exploded in clump of trees in Aiea Heights.

8:26 A.M. Breese received report of submarine in harbor.

8:27 A.M. 827 Sicard ceased firing, had expended three hundred rounds .30 cal. Machine gun ammunition.

8:30 A.M. Pennsy lighted fires under #4 boiler.

8:30 A.M. Conyngham reports another plane diving toward Ford Island from northeast shot down by combined fire of the nest.

8:30 A.M. Penna reports about five high bombing attacks observed to have passed over PENNA. One from port bow one from ahead one from ahead to starboard and two from astern from an altitude about two thousand feet.

8:30 A.M. Vireo brought down one enemy plane which landed in the vicinity of Hickam Field. Four hundred rounds of .30 cal. machine gun ammunition expended. One personnel casualty to U.S.S. Price (DE-332), an Edsall class Destroyer escort, Radioman, on telephone watch astern of vessel. Price returned to duty 10 December. No damage to vessel. Made ready to get underway.

8:30 A.M. Vestal prepared to get underway.

8:30 A.M. Mugford had five enemy planes in V formation pass directly overhead, making horizontal bombing attack.

8:30 A.M. Sumner checked fire.

8:30 A.M. Rigel observed fifteen Heavy bombers in 3-V formations, eight to ten thousand feet from southeast bombed BB's.

8:30 A.M. Whitney Issued ammunition and ordnance stores to destroyers alongside. Secured steam to destroyers. May have hit plane.

8:30 A.M. Hull Two Vee's high level bombers (ten thousand feet) were directly overhead and seen intermittently through the clouds. Hull opened fire with all guns. Formations broke up and dropped their bombs in cane field.

8:30 A.M. California opened fire on dive bombers with T5" and forward machine guns. They shot down one enemy dive bomber which crashed in flames.

8:30 A.M. Breese sighted conning towers of two submarines in north channel but could not open fire because of interior berth. Observed Monaghan proceed down channel at full speed to ram leading submarine which had just fired torpedo at Curtiss but missed. Monaghan dropped two depth charges and the submarine, about a 250 ton type arose upside down and sank.

8:30 A.M. Zane sighted strange submarine two hundred yards astern of Medusa Repair ship, moored in K-23. Guns would not bear as Zane was inboard ship.

8:30 A.M. Cassin received signal from Pennsylvania, Senior destroyer officer report on board.

8:30 A.M. Henley underway from buoy X-11 when a large bomb struck water one hundred fifty yards from port bow. Received signal "submarine in harbor." Macdonough directly ahead made depth charge attack and cleared at high speed. Henley was the third ship in sortie. After rounding Hospital Point, subjected to staffing attack by light bomber, coming up from astern and showing five distinct sources of machine gun fire from enemy plane, as plane passed ship. It was seen to crash offshore within a few minutes.

Another light bomber approached from starboard at two thousand feet and was taken under fire with another Destroyer. Close burst forced plane to dive, and it crashed into sea.

8:30 A.M. Downes opened fire with 5-inch, on blocks. Downes struck on after deck house by bombs.

8:30 A.M. Rigel Captain returned on board. Bomb struck astern and midway between piers 13 & 14. One hundred fifty small holes were blown into port quarter of Rigel above waterline.

8:30 A.M. Reid took the first group of enemy planes under fire with forward 5" and .50 caliber machine guns.

8:30 A.M. Outgoing To NPL RDO San Diego & NPM RDO Wailupe: One must have instantaneous relay for my dispatches.

8:30 A.M. COM-14 To NAS (Naval Air Station) Pearl: Hostile Japanese air attack X Hickam Field bombed X stay clear this area as long as gas permits X keep in contact this station.

8:30 A.M. 0832 California reported one enemy plane shot down over Ford Island.

8:32 A.M. 0832 Sicard Observed 4 flights horizontal bombers attacking battleships, followed by eight torpedo bombers. Oklahoma struck by several torpedoes, took heavy list to starboard and capsized. Arizona struck by torpedoes and heavy bomb.

8:32 A.M. Pyro observed enemy planes crash and burst into flame towards Barbers Point. Pilots bailed out. Observed damage to ship which consisted of broken steam line; repaired by ship's force.

8:35 A.M. Curtis ready to get underway. Sighted submarine periscope on starboard quarter, at a distance of seven hundred yards. Opened fire on submarine.

8:35 A.M. Sicard sent working party of twenty men to Cummings to handle ammunition, and four gunner's mates to New Orleans to assist her battery. Ten men had been previously detailed to Pennsylvania to assist damage control.

8:35 A.M. Bobolink moved out of nest and to first buoy. Observed Japanese plane crash near Hickam Field. Believe it was the result of minesweeper firing. Destroyer Preble reports first phase of attack completed.

8:36 A.M. COM-14 To ships present: Send boats to Ford Island.

8:38 A.M. Mugford and West Virginia burning. Arizona on fire. Tugs trying to pull overturned Oklahoma clear. U. S. S. Vestal clearing crew of Nevada.

8:40 A.M. California shaken by four near bomb hits and splintered considerably by fragments.

8:40 A.M. U.S.S. Nevada (BB-36) got underway to clear channel, but apparently was struck by a torpedo or a mine. A minute later two bombs fell but only one hit the Nevada. Fires and flooding were out of control and the crew attempted to manage them but to no avail. The Nevada had taken on too much water and sunk in the Harbor in shallow waters.

During the second attack a bomb was dropped on the forward part of Pennsylvania in dry-dock. Flames appeared from two destroyers in the same dock.

It was noted that another Japanese plane fell in the water and a bomb was seen falling close to the destroyers in floating dry-dock. One of the destroyers later caught on fire.

8:40 A.M. Curtiss witnessed enemy submarine surfaced and fired one torpedo up North Channel toward destroyers. Conning tower hit twice by gun #3.

8:40 A.M. Cummings opened fire to repel strafing attack. Dive bomber observed to veer away from ship with smoke trailing, passed over new boiler shop and disappeared in smoke.

8:40 A.M. Jarvis noted Nevada underway and standing out. Dive bombed, hit several times, and beached. Shaw hit and caught on fire in drydock. Two destroyers in drydock with Pennsylvania hit.

8:40 A.M. Trever ready for getting underway. Trever could not clear because other ships astern were clearing buoys D-3 and D-4. Enemy plane brought down vicinity of Pearl City. Second plane brought down two hundred yards off Beckoning Point.

8:42 A.M. Mugford and Vestal clear of Nevada.

0845 PHOENIX Ship ready to get underway.

8:43 A.M. Curtiss ceased firing on submarine and observed Monaghan drop two depth charges. Air bubbles and slick appeared.

8:45 A.M. Sicard observed attack broken off.

8:45 A.M. Vestal observed Arizona quarterdeck awash. With no steering gear Vestal got underway while tug pulled her bow away from

Arizona. Starting to list to starboard side Vestal was maneuvered into position with South end on McGrews Point bearing 30 distance 910 yds.

8:45 A.M. Mugford executed signal to get underway to Task Force One and Two. Tugs pulled Oglala clear of Helena.

8:45 A.M. California Commander Stone, executive officer, arrived and assumed command of California. Commanding Officer returned on board.

8:45 A.M. Cachalot Dive bomb and strafing attacks made by enemy.

8:45 A.M. Hull second attack. All attacks except one was broken up. One formation of three planes continued on. Two of these were shot down. One was shot down USS Dobbin (AD-3), a Destroyer Tender, and one by the next of ships. Two bombs landed astern of next, close to side of Dobbin.

8:45 A.M. Castor ready to get underway.

8:47 A.M. Blue underway upon execution of signal to get underway from berth X-7. Maintained fire on enemy planes with main battery and machine guns while steaming out of harbor. Four planes fired on with main battery were later seen to go down in smoke. It is claimed that two of these planes were definitely shot down by this vessel. One was seen to crash in field on Waipio Peninsula and the second crashed into crane on stern of USS Curtiss. Two planes that dove over the ship were fired on by the .50 caliber machine guns. It is claimed that one of these planes, seen to crash near Pan American Dock, was shot down by this vessel.

8:50 A.M. Mugford and West Virginia listed heavily to port.

8:50 A.M. Zane reports Monaghan approached, and depth charged submarine. Enemy plane brought down flying over nest, struck deperming station.

8:50 A.M. Sumner dispatched ship's boats to Ford Island to assist in hauling ammunition.

8:50 A.M. Downes hit again by bombs and set on fire. Ship ordered to Abandoned ship.

8:50 A.M. COMDESFLOT 1 To DESPLOT 1: Desdiv TWO establish Offshore patrol.

8:51 A.M. Mugford executed signal to get underway and sortie which is an attack made by troops coming out from a position of defense according to plan E-S.

8:51 A.M. COM-14 To CINPAC. Enemy Submarine reported in Pearl Harbor for Sector Commanders.

8:54 A.M. Mugford attack started again from North.

8:55 A.M. Conyngham fired at plane strafing ahead and astern.

8:55 A.M. 1017 underway from Buoy D-3 Middle Loch Ramsey, Breese. Gamble and Montgomery opened fire with AA.

8:55 A.M. Mugford and Nevada underway. Dense smoke over Ford Island. A tanker was towed clear of Ford Island.

8:55 A.M. Pruitt observed about ten planes made high altitude horizontal bombing.

8:55 A.M. Whitney observed second air attack by Japanese bombing planes.

8:55 A.M. USS Ralph Talbot (DD-390) was moored bow to southward to buoy X-11 with Patterson to port and Henley to starboard.

8:55 A.M. Ramsey underway proceeding out of harbor. Believe Ramsey is responsible for shooting down plane with .50 cal. Assumed antisubmarine patrol on clearing channel.

8:57 A.M. CTF 9 To all ships: Enemy submarine in North Channel.

8:59 A.M. UNKNOWN To CINCPAC: Ten aircraft approaching Pearl Harbor from Southwest.

9:00 A.M. TRACY reports high altitude bombers raced overhead in several waves. One bomb fell in slip between stern of Rigel and Cummings at Berth 15.

9:00 A.M. Mugford attack started again from the South. Army planes taking off from Hickam Field.

9:00 A.M. Rigel Executive Officer returned on board. Traffic congestion delayed all hands. The one exception to all hands was Lt. H. E. Morgan who did not return until 8:00 A.M. next morning. Lt. Morgan's behavior is being investigated.

9:00 A.M. Sicard observed dive bombers from Southeast attack ships moored to Navy Yard docks, followed by waves of dive and horizontal bombers on ships at Ford Island and docks.

9:00 A.M. Oglala approaching 40' list to port. Ordered all hands abandon ship. Only gun crews and Cominbatfor remained.

9:00 A.M. Phoenix Formation of eleven planes passed over fleet on heading 070. Approximate altitude 10,000 feet. Planes appeared to be painted silver, Expended fifty rounds of 5". No apparent damage to planes. There were two flights of this nature. Time of second cannot be approximated. Expended fifty rounds of 5".

9:00 A.M. Honolulu enemy bomber sighted flying directly towards this ship from direction Merry Point with an altitude of 1,000 feet. Was seen to swerve to its left, pass over the Navy Yard, smoking, losing altitude and appeared to crash near Naval Hospital. This plane was under the fire of several ships. Including the port 5" and machine gun batteries of the Honolulu. Damage to enemy observed, one torpedo plane shot down between berth 21, submarine Base, one torpedo plane shot down between berth 21 BB. (Note: Damage listed above is at unknown times.)

9:00 A.M. Tautog observed planes approaching in direction Hickam Field high in southwest and mostly obscured by clouds. Approximately eighteen planes turned left over Hickam Field and made dive bombing attacks on ships in yard. Dive appeared slow and bombs released were very low. One plane observed out of control in flames. Scattered enemy planes observed until 11:30 A.M. Most dive bombers appeared to drop two bombs each.

9:00 A.M. California one bomb, possibly 15" projectile with tale vanes, struck California abreast casemate one, frame 59, penetrated to second deck and exploded rupturing forward and after bulkheads of A-611 and overhead into A-705. Armored hatch to machine shop badly sprung and couldn't be closed, resulting in serious fire.

9:00 A.M. Breese projectile from Breese 3" AA battery struck dive bomber which had just attacked Curtiss. Forward section of plane with motor landed on North side of Waipio Peninsula.

9:00 A.M. Ralph Talbot underway. While enroute to entrance expended 150 rounds 5"/38 cal. and 1500 rounds .50 cal. Observed two planes crash and another start to smoke badly. Two enemy planes dove low over bridge and was hit by our .50 cal. machine guns. Plane crashed along shore Pearl City abeam of us. Used after 5" guns to fire on plane attacking Curtiss.

9:00 A.M. Dewey second wave attack started by light bombers lasting ten minutes under fire by Dewey throughout attack.

0**9:00 A.M.** Patterson underway and stood out of harbor. No damage sustained by Patterson.

9:00 A.M. Solace ship underway and shifted from Berth X4 to Berth X13. No material or personnel damage to ship proper.

9:00 A.M. Bobolink observed suspicious sign of Japanese submarine and signaled to destroyers, but signal apparently not seen.

9:00 A.M. Bobolink observed three flights of high altitude bombers approaching from due south to north. Seven planes in each flight, altitude about 17,000 feet. One flight dropped bombs on Hickam, second flight passed directly over coal docks and dropped bombs further up in yard; third flight passed over West Loch, one plane dropping bombs near entrance while others maintained course and dropped them beyond Ford Island.

9:00 A.M. Raleigh dive bomber attack came in which was met with warm reception. One bomb hit ship a glancing blow going through carpenter shop and oil tank, piercing the skin below water line, and finally detonating on bottom of harbor. Plane machine gunned ship also. Steam raised in 3 and 4 firerooms and pumps started. Five bombing planes under fire were observed to crash close aboard.

9:00 A.M. Honolulu saw five high altitude bombers at 12,000 to 15,000 feet appear. All bombed Pearl Harbor and Ford Island Area.

9:00 A.M. Rigel saw fifteen dive bombers 6,000 to 10 thousand feet from North that attacked DDs and Nevada.

9:00 A.M. Solace got underway and shifted from berth X-4, near DOB- BIN and destroyers to berth X-13 in the clear. Made boat trips to West Virginia to bring back casualties.

9:00 A.M. Dobbins fired upon enemy plane headed astern of ship. Japanese plane crashed upon trees in Navy Yard.

9:00 A.M. Oglala capsized alongside 10/10 dock.

9:00 A.M.-9:15 A.M. Phoenix five bombing attack on ships berth northern side of Ford Island. Attack was made at about 30 angle, opposed with AA and MG batteries. Expended twenty rounds of 5". One plane disintegrated by DD fire.

9:00 A.M.-9:30 A.M. Phoenix effected periodic fire on planes delivering low-level bombing attack on navy yard and ships berth there.

9:01 A.M. Cummings observed twelve scattered planes over Ford Island; air raid resumed. Opened fire with main battery on horizontal bombers approaching over Navy Yard industrial section.

9:02 A.M. Mugford observed formation of planes sighted to South. Decks of Arizona and West Virginia level with water. Dense smoke pouring from Nevada.

9:03 A.M. Dolphin reports another attack from higher altitude.

9:03 A.M. Outgoing To MIDWAY: Pearl Harbor bombed no indication direction attack take off attempt locate Japanese Forces.

9:03 A.M. Outgoing To WAKE: Pearl bombed by Japanese be on alert.

9:05 A.M. Curtiss observed one of three planes pulling out of dive was hit by Curtiss and crashed into #1 crane. Tank exploded and plane burned on Boat Deck.

9:05 A.M. Sumner fired on wave of dive bombers approaching Navy Yard. Dive bombers also attacked Hickam Field and Battleships no hits when firing. On latter planes. Observed light dive bomber with conspicuous red tail zig-zag over Navy Yard as if observing casualties at end of phase.

9:05 A.M. Tracy attacked by approximately ten dive bombers from direction of the sun, which indicated drydock as objective. Group of six, three and nine planes observed at altitude of 8,000 to 10,000 feet. Bomb seen to fall between berths 13 and 15 in slip. Tracy gig damaged by fragmentation, no casualties.

9:05 A.M. Preble observed about thirty dive bombers make second attack in twin- motored monoplanes. Observed one bomb fall in slip twenty-five yards on star-board quarter.

Observed a bomb fall astern of Honolulu in berth B-21. Observed numerous bombs fall in vicinity of drydock area.

9:05 A.M. Whitney observed one Japanese plane fall down in flames on hilltop, bearing northeast, true.

9:06 A.M. Pennsylvania observed the second attack coming in slightly on port bow. It dropped bombs on ships in drydock. One heavy bomb hit the destroyer Downes in dock ahead of Pennsylvania, and one hit dock approximately abreast frame 20 while one hit the boat deck of the Pennsylvania a few feet abaft gun #7. This bomb passed through boat deck and detonated in #5 gun #9 casemate.

Fifth bomb believed to have struck water outside of dock. Observed plane crash in hospital grounds Observers claim to have destroyed six enemy planes. Consider two were hit by Pennsylvania.

9:06 A.M. Mugford observed Japanese planes diving on Ford Island from southeast. Nevada standing down south channel.

9:07 A.M. Pruitt observed strafing and light bombing attack, plus heavy horizontal bombing attack from about 10,000 feet made on ships and Ford Island. One bomb hit close to stern of Rigel.

9:07 A.M. Pennsylvania bomb hit on dock and cut yard power, subsequently power on the ship was taken from storage batteries, meanwhile, fire main pressure cut off.

9:07 A.M. OUTGOING ALL HANDS: Cease firing on U.S. B-17's attempting to land at Hickam.

9:08 A.M. Conyngham reports one plane attacking on starboard bow shot down by nest and crashed in Pearl City.

9:08 A.M. Com 14 to ASP Do not fire on our planes coming in.

9:08 A.M. Nevada attack slackened.

9:09 A.M. Mugford bomb dropped some four hundred yards on Mugford port bow. Ship in repair basin hit.

9:10 A.M. Perry at Mine Division FOUR underway at intervals and stood out to take offshore patrol duty.

9:10 A.M. SECNAV to ALNAV Execute WPL FORTY SIX against Japan.

9:10 A.M. Dive bombers attacked ships at Pier 19; bombs fell in water ahead and astern within two and a half yards of Cummings.

9:10 A.M. Dobbin attacked by three enemy planes. Three bombs dropped all near misses. Fragments struck stern of ship injuring #4 3" AA gun crew. Three killed, two injured. Damage. Small holes through decks, bulkheads, booms, #1 MWB hull damaged beyond repair.

Fifth bomb believed to have struck water outside of dock. Observed plane crash in hospital grounds Observers claim to have destroyed six enemy planes. Consider two were hit by Pennsylvania.

9:10 A.M. Blue passed channel entrance buoys and set course 120 true. Proceeded to sector three to patrol station.

9:10 A.M. Rigel observed ten to twelve dive bombers from the south that attacked ships in Repair Basin with bombs and mach. guns.

9:10 A.M. Phoenix observed second bombing attack on Battleships. Expended sixty rounds of 5". After planes came out of dive and turned towards berth C-6, planes were brought under fire of MG battery.

9:10 A.M. Vestal anchored in thirty-five feet of water. Soundings and draft readings showed ship settling at and listing to starboard Draft aft increased to twenty-seven foot list to six and one half feet. Commanding Officer of the Vestal decided to ground ship.

9:10 A.M. Conyngham opened fire on horizontal bombers approaching from ahead and from direction of Schofield.

9:10 A.M. Thornton observed second wave of dive bombing attack commenced and ended at 9:17 A.M. Throughout the entire period there was horizontal bombing in various Pearl Harbor areas.

9:11 A.M. Mugford observed horizontal Japanese bombers passed overhead.

9:12 A.M. Pyro observed dive bombers approach from port bow, at an altitude five thousand feet and release bombs. Bombs landed on concrete dock twelve feet from ship's side amidships. Penetrated dock exploding underneath and jarring ship.

9:12 A.M. Curtiss reports group of planes under heavy fire attacked. During attack one bomb hit stern mooring buoy. One fell short, one over one hit ship starboard side of boat deck, passed through Carpenter Shop and Radio Repair Shop, entered Hangar, and detonated on Main Deck.

Explosion destroyed bulk heads, deck. etc., within radius of thirty feet. Equipment destroyed in Hangar. Handling Room etc. One plane shot down one thousand yards on port bow and fifteen hundred yards on port beam.

Another plane shot on port beam landing in water off Pan Am Air dock. One plane reported crashed in cane field astern and one forward of ship.

9:12 A.M. Mugford observed heavy black smoke coming from Shaw in floating drydock.

9:13 A.M. Mugford and Nevada stopped south side of south channel.

9:13 A.M. Preble attack completed. No damage. No casualties sustained by this ship.

9:15 A.M. Large explosion on Downes.

9:15 A.M. Helm observed a small enemy fighter that had approached ship from astern in medium glide and dropped two bombs, which exploded in water about fifty yards off port bow and twenty yards of starboard bow.

After that, the machine guns opened fire but did not hit plane. Shock shorted relay to steering (which had just been repaired) and damaged gyro rotor. Choke coils tubes and resistors in sound gear burned out, echo ranging inoperative. Seams below waterline on starboard side forward sprung. A-15, A-301 A-401, and A 402 flooded. These compartments closed off and pumped out during afternoon.

Food Service smoke generators jumped track, breaking airline connection.

9:15 A.M. Captain Bunkley returned to California and assumed command.

9:15 A.M. Nevada 5" A. A. battery fired on enemy planes to eastward. Nevada suffered at least six bomb hits and one torpedo hit.

9:15 A.M. Mugford had thick black smoke coming from drydock.

9:15 A.M. Tracy Commanding Officer returned aboard and found 2 .50 cal. machine guns mounted and ready. Two dive bombers attacked out of the sun.

One plane pulling out over subbase and flying low over building 155 crashed in flames in vicinity of hospital point after salvo by Cummings. Plane appeared to be a type 95 dive bomber Planes appeared to be at about three thousand feet to seaward of Hickam with eighteen planes in formation type V.

9:17 A.M. Pruitt observed low flying pursuit planes strafing with machine gun fire on ships moored in the vicinity of Berth 18. Observers on this ship believe many high altitude horizontal bombs either failed to explode or landed outside the harbor area where they could not be observed. An indeterminate number of fighters took part in the raid, with approximately thirty bombers. Approaches were made on a steady course and all horizontal bombing was made in close formation at about ten thousand feet.

The four cruisers and light minelayers in the Navy Yard were strafed several times by low flying planes but not a single bomb appeared to have been aimed at those ships. Small caliber fire of minelayers brought down one Japanese plane.

9:17 A.M. Breese cleared nest and proceeded down channel.

9:20 A.M. Cummings fired on a light bomber. Plane observed smoking heavily as it flew out of sight to south-westward.

9:20 A.M. Honolulu observed low winged dive bombers from South to Southeast, four hundred feet pullout. Two bombers bombed industrial and drydock areas. One bomb (clearly visible on its descent of two hundred fifty pounds, passed through edge of concrete dock, angle of descent forty-five, and exploded underwater between ship and dock.

9:20 A.M. Damage to Honolulu. Oil tanks various, decks bulged in magazines, various leaks sprung, and decks slightly buckled, power lease to turret #2 grounded, turret #1 partially grounded, mercury thrown out of gyros, fore and aft, rangefinders, main batteries drained both fore and aft.

9:20 A.M. More Japanese planes from northwest.

9:20 A.M. Conyngham opened fire on plane diving from port side of nest. No personnel or material damage.

9:20 A.M. Pennsylvania had flooding of drydock commence. Both destroyers heavily on fire. Fire being transmitted to fire on water and dock which set fire to paint on starboard side of Pennsylvania.

No hose available for fighting fire on Downes. Available hose being used on Cassin.

9:20 A.M. Outgoing ALL HANDS: Reported that enemy ships have red dot on bottom of fuselage.

9:21 A.M. Outgoing COMBATFOR: To ALL SHIPS PRESENT: Get underway immediately.

9:23 A.M. Mugford and Patterson standing out.

9:23 A.M. Outgoing COMBATFOR TO COMCRUBATFOR: Cruisers proceed as soon as possible. Landline send over boats to capsized battleship Oklahoma.

9:24 A.M. Received COMSUBSCOFOR TO COMSUBDIV 43: Assume service ammunition readiness condition ONE be prepared to attack on information furnished later.

9:24 A.M. Received Communications from COM14: All planes approaching from Fox George and Easy.

9:25 A.M. California's ship's plane 205 capsized and sunk while being removed to avoid gasoline fire hazard.

9:25 A.M. Wasmuth reports second phase of attack as dive bombers and torpedo planes approached from westerly direction. Scored hits on several planes and shot down one plane which crashed on Waipio Peninsula near Middle Loch. This plane should be credited to James Patrick Hammon, seaman first, class, U. S. Navy.

9:25 A.M. Gamble observed one Japanese plane shot down by AX fire, falling in water on port beam about one thousand yards away from ship. Believed shot down by ROBERTS, W. L., BM-2c, USS GAMBLE port machine gunner (#2 machine gun) .50 cal., and JOOS, H. W., GM-3c., USS GAMBLE (#1 machine gun) starboard.

9:25 A.M. Mugford observed white smoke pouring from amidship on Arizona.

9:26 A.M. Outgoing CTF 1: Battleships remain in port until further orders. Send all destroyers to sea and destroy enemy submarines. Follow them by all cruisers to join Halsey. Unknown Fire at will

9:27 A.M. Received COM 14: Aircraft coming from Barbers Point twenty or thirty miles. Flash: Enemy planes appear to be massing around Easy. Enemy planes coming from Wheeler Field.

9:27 A.M. Curtiss after engine room out of commission and evacuated.

9:27 A.M. Received RDO San Francisco to AS: USAT CYNTHIA OLSEN sent distress reports enemy submarine Lat. 33 R 42 N Long 145 R 29 W.

9:28 A.M. Mugford shot down enemy plane after it pulled out from dive on port bow. Altitude two hundred feet. With forward 50 caliber M. G. The plane was a dive bomber.

9:28 A.M. Received COMAIRBATFOR TO CINCPAC: 220P planes to arrive Pearl about 8:20 A.M.

9:30 A.M. Mugford and Oglala going over to port. Personnel abandoned ship and getting on dock.

9:30 A.M. Received COMSUBSCOFOR TO THRESHER, GUDGEON & LITCHFIELD: Assume service ammunition readiness condition ONE x remain in present position x report position.

9:30 A.M. Received Curtiss to CINCPAC: Unable to sortie because of damage. After Oglala sank her crew were pooled out and sent to various units of the Fleet to assist ships in maintaining their batteries.

9:30 A.M. Gamble got underway and cleared mooring buoy. Reports Division commenced getting underway. U. S. S. Breese underway.

9:30 A.M. Enemy planes strafed Castor and Neosho. Detailed men to handle U.S.S. Neosho (AO-23) a Navy fleet Oiler, lines astern of Castor.

9:30 A.M. Trever underway, standing out of entrance. Observed Perry fire at enemy submarine and Monaghan ramming and dropping depth charge.

9:30 A.M. Tennessee observed enemy planes coming in on port beam. West Virginia gangway still burning.

9:30 A.M. Helm shifted steering motor power to diesel generator: regained bridge control of steering.

9:30 A.M. California fire broke out on main deck, starboard side of "F" Division compartment and casemates 3, 5, and 7.

9:30 A.M. Breese Lookout reported periscope off Coal Docks but could not be observed from bridge or picked up by supersonics.

9:30 A.M. Dobbin reports attacks appeared to have been discontinued.

9:30 A.M. Whitney reports second air attack completed.

9:30 A.M. Pennsylvania observed explosions on destroyers commence, in floating dry-dock ahead of Pennsylvania.

9:32 A.M. Wasmuth underway following Trever on orders from Lt. Commander, L M. LeHardy, Commanding Officer, Zane and S. O. P. Mine Division 4.

9:33 A.M. Received COM 14: Flash: planes coming in from George.

9:35 A.M. Received Raleigh to CINCPAC: Two fire rooms and engine room and stern compartment flooded, water damage under control at present x unable to get underway.

9:35 A.M. Received Chicago to CRUSCOFOR: Japanese submarines reported inside and outside Pearl.

9:35 A.M. Received ARMY Headquarters: Flash: Fishing boat one mile off Manakuli.

9:36 A.M. Received CPW2 TO CPW 1: We are being attacked by fifteen Japanese planes.

9:36 A.M. Curtiss fire under control.

9:37 A.M. Wasmuth Lieutenant J. W. Leverton, Jr., USN, Executive Officer, reported: Friendly aircraft coming from toward Barbers Point twenty or thirty planes.

9:37 A.M. Gamble observed Japanese planes attack near main channel entrance.

9:37 A.M. Mugford observed explosion on destroyer ahead of the U. S. S. Pennsylvania in drydock

9:38 A.M. Mugford reports Japanese subs inside and outside of Pearl Harbor.

9:40 A.M. Wasmuth Lieutenant. Commander D. M. Agnew, USN, CO USS Trever reported aboard. Proceeded out of Pearl Harbor and took up patrol off entrance.

9:40 A.M. Bagley ship underway from dock. Material Damage: Broken windows and light globes and glasses on reduction gears causing loss of lubricating oil. Personnel damage with four men slightly injured.

9:40 A.M. Tennessee reports wounded being removed from the West Virginia. Oklahoma upside down. Bow blown away on Arizona. Destroyers getting underway on other side of Ford Island. Fire either on Argonne or dock. Air attack coming in on starboard bow. West Virginia on fire from turret one to bow. Flames up as high as foretop. Fire on port quarter (oil on water).

9:40 A.M. Bagley underway from dock and proceeded around north side Ford Island under belief that other channel was blocked. Because of defective bilge keel, ship was ordered to patrol offshore area and did not accompany Task Force 8. No damage to ship.

9:40 A.M. Nevada grounded off Hospital Point.

9:41 A.M. Pennsylvania observed warheads on Downes explode covering area with debris. Section of torpedo tube, weighing about one thousand pounds landed on Pennsylvania forecastle. Fire brought under control before serious damage resulted.

Cassin rolled over on Downes. It was noted by everyone participating in action that after an hour or more heavy thirst was experienced requiring considerable drinking water. This confirms the necessity of having water at all battle stations.

9:42 A.M. Breese cleared channel entrance with degaussing gear cut in and took station as offshore patrol in section 3.

9:42 A.M. Received COM 14 to ASP & NAVSHORE ACTIVITIES: brief concentrations reported twenty-five miles south by southeast of Barbers Point x not definite.

9:42 A.M. Mugford and Bagley underway.

9:43 A.M. U.S.S. Tern (AM-31,) a minesweeper, underway from alongside dock to pick up survivors in harbor. Received forty-seven survivors

9:45 A.M. Dewey observed third wave of attack started by dive bombers. Dobbin and Desdiv One were target with three or four planes attacking. One bomb hit close aboard starboard quarter and one hit water between Hull and Dewey astern. No damage. Guns 1 and 2 firing when not blanked by Dobbin. It is believed that Desdiv ONE destroyed two planes. Ammunition expended; seventy-six rounds 5", thirteen hundred rounds .50 cal.

9:45 A.M. Cachalot joined in fire against enemy bombers. No damage received. Nearest enemy bomb dropped twenty feet starboard quarter and did not explode. Nearest torpedo passed one hundred yards astern.

9:45 A.M. Mugford and Oglala capsized to port.

9:45 A.M. Mugford observed Japanese planes in from Southwest low.

9:47 A.M. Mugford and Honolulu underway.

9:48 A.M. Tennessee observed planes coming in on starboard bow; did not know whether enemy or friendly. Ship will not get underway until further orders from Engineering Department, stand by. Destroyer, from Navy Yard, getting underway. Unidentified ship in Pearl Harbor down by stern.

9:50 A.M. Vestal grounded.

9:50 A.M. Blue has good sound contact on enemy submarine. Maneuvered to attack and dropped four depth charges. Regained sound contact on same submarine.

Dropped two depth charges. Investigated and observed large oil slick and air bubbles rising to surface. It is felt that this submarine was definitely sunk.

Obtained third contact on a submarine that was apparently headed for U.S.S. St Louis, which was at the time heading out on course approximately 150 true, at high speed. Two depth charges dropped, and upon return noticed large oil slick on surface. It is claimed that one, and possibly two, submarines were sunk.

9:50 A.M. Outgoing two enemy carriers reported thirty miles southwest Barbers Point, (Sent to CTF 8).

9:51 A.M. Tennessee reports lighter alongside starboard beam on fire (ammunition lighter, top blown out. Can see no ammunition on it.).

9:51 A.M. Received COM 14 to ASP: Two planes seen dropping heavy charges off harbor entrance which did not explode; think they are mines,

9:52 A.M. Outgoing battleships remain in part probable channel mined.

9:54 A.M. Tennessee observed bow of Maryland on fire.

9:54 A.M. Received SOPA San Diego to ASP HAWAIIAN AREA: Los Angeles Harbor Air Defense Plan Number One effective. Unknown SIGNAL TOWER

The following ships have left Pearl Harbor: Dale, St. Louis, Henley, Phelps, Ramsey, Wasmuth, Patterson, Montgomery.

9:55 A.M. Gamble temporarily anchored, astern of USS Medusa (AR-1) a repair ship.

9:55 A.M. Tennessee still using fire hose on ammunition lighter. Fire seems to under control.

9:55 A.M. Mugford commenced receiving fuel oil from the yard line. Perry and Gamble standing out.

9:56 A.M. Tennessee observed Solace getting underway.

9:57 A.M. Mugford and California listing to port.

9:58 A.M. Mugford BB's order to remain in port.

9:58 A.M. Tennessee observed the fire on bow of Maryland. Was under control. Superstructure on West Virginia on fire-four or five men trapped, trying to escape by crane.

File (oil on water) at stern of Tennessee was out. Fire very close to D-310 M. 1000 Cummings opened fire to repel horizontal bombing attack from the Southward. One horizontal bomber observed to lose its wing. Cummings gun captain #4 claimed a hit.

10:00 A.M. Whitney reports Reid and Selfridge underway.

10:02 A.M. California oil fire on surface of water enveloped ship starting many fires, particularly intense one on forecastle. Captain Bunkley, with approval of Commander Battle Force ordered ship to be abandoned temporarily due to enveloping oil fire on surface of water.

10:02 A.M. Tennessee Flood D-310-M (D-306-M and D-312-M also flooded, not isolated).

10:03 A.M. Mugford observed Japanese planes reported dropping mines in channel.

10:05 A.M. Gamble underway proceeding out of channel.

10:05 A.M. Fort Shafter observed some heavy bombs dropped at entrance of Pearl Harbor that did not explode. Think they are mines.

10:05 A.M. SOPA San Diego go to ASP San Diego: San Diego Harbor Air Defense Plan Number ONE effective.

10:05 A.M. Mugford and U. S. S. Shaw in floating dry-dock exploded. Main engines and two boilers of Mugford ready to get underway.

10:08 A.M. Tennessee observed Arizona aflame all over.

10:10 A.M. UNKNOWN To RDO WAILUPE: This vessel and 4 DM in Southwest fifty-two enemy carriers in sight. (Rec'd by phone).

10:10 A.M. Reid got underway on four boilers. No damage or casualties.

10:10 A.M. Phoenix got underway, but returned to Berth C-6 on receiving orders not to sortie.

10:10 A.M. Sumner fired two rounds at bomber on port beam, altitude 8,000 no hits. Also fired .50 caliber machine guns, two and four. 1010 TENNESSEE Observed planes approaching from starboard beam; did not come in.

10:11 A.M. CPW 2 To DEWT: Report CPW 2 for duty.

10:13 A.M. Mugford, U. S. S. Schley and Allen ready to get underway. UNKNOWN VP-24 To CPW 2 Eight men of war Lat. 21.10 Long 160. 16 course 090 degrees UNKNOWN USCG 400 To CG RDO STATION: Report immediately to Commander Honolulu Base.

10:14 A.M. Com 14 was Lualualei NAD damaged.

10:15 A.M. CTF 9 To COMPATRON 21 Search Sector 000 to 300 Japanese Carriers

10:15 A.M. Gamble shifted .30 cal. A. A. machine guns to top of pilot house on fire control platform.

10:18 A.M. CINCPAC To CTF 8,12, 3 Search from Pearl very limited account maximum twelve VP searching X Some indication enemy force northwest Oahu X Addressees operate as directed Com Task Force 8 to intercept and attack enemy composition enemy force unknown.

10:18 A.M. CTF 8 Is Ford Island available re service and rearm carrier planes in case Tennessee reports Arizona looks as if she is on the bottom. Word passed for the 5th division to lay aft to relieve fire party.

10:20 A.M. CINCPAC To CTF One: Do not send any more cruisers to Sea. 1020 CTG 1.9 To ALL Air Coms Patwing (Patrol Wing) 1 & 2. Observe approach Doctrine when near Oahu.

10:20 A.M. Mugford AND U. S. S. Jarvis cleared starboard side.

10:20 A.M. Attack group of fifteen VSB's with 1,000 lb. bombs each dispatched to position thirty miles south Barber's Point where numerous reports had been received of enemy carriers and other forces; no contact. CINC informed Comtaskfor EIGHT depended on Pearl Harbor for scouting information. This in order maintain carrier striking group in readiness.

10:21 A.M. Gamble cleared channel entrance. Eight depth charges were armed, and the ship commenced offshore and anti-submarine patrol off Pearl Harbor entrance.

10:22 A.M. Mugford Navy MT's standing out.

10:23 A.M. Wasmuth dropped one depth charge on suspicious water, set- ting two hundred feet, results negative.

10:23 A.M. Mugford floating in dry dock sinking.

10:24 A.M. Tennessee reports torpedo boats leaving harbor.

10:27 A.M. Tennessee reports people coming from West Virginia on board Tennessee by way of a five inch gun.

10:27 A.M. Mugford A transport and Cummings underway standing out.

10:28 A.M. NAS PEARL To CTF 8: Your 2023 Affirmative. (Ref: Is Ford Island available re service and rearm carrier planes in ease necessity).

10:28 A.M. Pennsylvania power on ship taken on two generators.

10:30 A.M. Castor transferred ammunition to Neosho for use of that vessel.

10:30 A.M. Henley visual signal from Trever reported the Henley's captain and executive officer on board that vessel.

10:30 A.M. Blue upon completion of attacks, Blue screened St. Louis.

10:30 A.M. Sicard observed attack break off. Mustered crew, no injuries, or casualties.

10:30 A.M. Phoenix got underway and started out north of channel. Received message from Tennessee from CINCPAC "Do not Sortie". Turned around in channel and started back to berth C.-6. On receipts of orders from Comcrubatfor proceeded via south channel and completed sortie and joined COMTASKFOR ONE.

10:30 A.M. Mugford fuel oil barge moored starboard quarter.

10:30 A.M. Pennsylvania sent motor launches to West Loch for more ammunition.

10:31 A.M. UNKNOWN This vessel and 4 DM in southwest S2 *NO* enemy carriers in sight.

10:32 A.M. Tennessee observes Arizona abandoning ship. Repair II report all C&R soundings normal. Repair IV report all soundings normal. Pull circuit L28 at aft. Distribution Board. Mr. Teague says hatches cannot be opened from inside wardroom country too hot.

10:32 A.M. SIGNAL TOWER To CINCPAC: These ships underway but have not cleared the entrance yet: Detroit, Jarvis, Perry, New Orleans, Gamble, Chew.

10:33 A.M. COMBATSHIPS Be ready to repel repeated air attacks.

10:33 A.M. CTF 3, CTF 8 To ASP; Enemy submarines reported ten miles south Barber's point.

10:33 A.M. Tennessee 6 down by stern from flooding of D-306, D-312 M.

10:36 A.M. Tennessee Unit 2, Repair I, combating fire in W. R. Country. Dead man forward of conning tower, sent stretcher party.

10:36 A.M. Wasmuth dropped second depth charge on suspicious water, setting 200 feet, bearing 217 , distance 3.4 miles from Pearl Harbor entrance buoys. Brought up large quantities of oil, but no wreckage.

10:40 A.M. Yune 8 bearing (BILATERAL) 357 or 178 T from Heeia. Yune 8 is Comcardivs (AKAGI).

10:40 A.M. COMDESRON 3 Underway accordance signal from tower, and oral orders. Joined anti sub patrol operating off entrance. Made two Sound contacts, dropped' 3 and 2 depth charges. Oil observed on water but no conclusive evidence of submarine loss.

10:40 A.M. COMBASEFOR To COMDINRON 2: Sweep South channel from East Loch to entrance magnetic and moored mines.

10:40 A.M. Mugford commenced receiving fuel from oil barge in addition to oil from yard line.

10:40 A.M. Tracy reported Cummings underway after returning all Tracy men. Ten men sent to help fight fire in California.

10:42 A.M. Combatfor To Capt NYD: The California is on fire inside. Probably two tugs with fire equipment could save her.

10:42 A.M. Downes fire on Cassin brought under control.

10:46 A.M. COMBATSHIPS To BATSHIPS IN COMPANY: All battleships sent pilots and aviation personnel to Ford Island immediately.

10:46 A.M. CTF 8 DF bearings indicate enemy carrier bearing 178 from Barber's point

10:48 A.M. Tennessee To CINCPAC: Tennessee 30% damage. California has been sunk. Doubtful checking.

10:50 A.M. Tern proceeded to put out fire on USS Arizona. Shifted over to West Virginia by orders from Maryland.

10:42 A.M. Downes fire on Cassin brought under control.

10:46 A.M. COMBATSHIPS To BATSHIPS IN COMPANY: All battleships sent pilots and aviation personnel to Ford Island immediately.

10:46 A.M. CTF 8 DF bearings indicate enemy carrier bearing 178 from Barber's point

10:48 A.M. Tennessee To CINCPAC: Tennessee 30% damage. California has been sunk. Doubtful checking.

10:50 A.M. Tern proceeded to put out fire on USS Arizona. Shifted over to West Virginia by orders from Maryland.

10:51 A.M. CPW 1 To Plane 2 VP 14: Search sector 310 to 320. Take due caution. Unknown CTF 8 To CINCPAC: CINCPAC 2012 Acknowledge.

10:53 A.M. Minneapolis to CINCPAC: Minneapolis center area VICTOR ONE.

10:55 A.M. CTF 8 To CINCPAC: Am depending on Pearl for scouting information.

10:55 A.M. CTF 8 CTF 8 launched six VOS to search sector O00-045 to 150 miles.

10:55 A.M. Sumner fired two rounds 3" at plane dead ahead, altitude 8,000. No hits. Fired all 50 caliber.

10:56 A.M. Mugford observed Japanese planes attacking from North. (Note: These are apparently friendly planes).

10:58 A.M. Mugford observed numerous explosions from West Virginia and Arizona.

10:58 A.M. Tennessee observed Naval Air Station planes in air.

10:58 A.M. PATRON 23 To CPW ONE: Investigating suspicious vessel 21 00, 150 50.

11:00 A.M. Tracy observed Japanese have definitely withdrawn.

11:00 A.M. COM 14 TO NAS PEARL. CPW 2: Hawaiian Air Force contemplates moving headquarters; MUX lines will be kept in commission. UNKNOWN COMBASEFOR, C0MINRON TWO to COM 14: Sweep South channel from East Loch to entrance magnetic and moored mines.

11:00 A.M. Tennessee Repair II told to open drain valve and core valve in GSK, Valves to Sick Bay. Enemy plane coming in on bow. All hands not engaged in fighting fire seek cover.

11:00 A.M. Helm Sound listening watch heard screws on starboard quarter. Ship circled for attack but lost control. No depth charges dropped.

11:00 A.M. Sicard observed horizontal bombing attack.

11:00 A.M. Mugford fire appeared to be under control on Nevada.

11:03 A.M. Tennessee observed destroyer putting to sea (other side of Ford Island). Gasoline stowage filled with C02.

11:03 A.M. VP 23 #11 To CPW2: Ships investigated two subs unknown nationality course 271 submerged on my approach.

11:05 A.M. NAS Kaneohe To CINCPAC: Ship nationality unknown ten miles off Kahana Point.

11:05 A.M. To ASP, Info CTF 8 All ships departing Pearl organize as TASKFORCE ONE UNDIVIDED Comdesbatfor assume command report CTF 8.

11:05 A.M. To ASP this Circuit: Enemy planes coming for Pearl Harbor from South.

11:08 A.M. Breese received reports Motor Torpedo Boat sighted periscope

11:08 A.M. St. Louis To CINCPAC: Formed attack group St. Louis, Lamson, Phelps, I am proceeding to locate *ENEMY*.

11:08 A.M. CPW 2 To PATRON 23 Empty tanker no guns showing identity unknown lat. 2100 Long. 259 59.

11:10 A.M. NYD OPERATIONS To CINCPAC: NYD Operations reports another air raid expected within twenty minutes.

11:10 A.M. Sicard observed horizontal diving attack completed.

11:15 A.M. Breese dropped two depth charges on spot indicated with no apparent results. Bearings: Barber's Point 297 (t), and Hickam Tower

11:18 A.M. NAS Kaneohe Bay to CINCPAC: Ship nationality unknown ten miles off Kahana Point.

11:19 A.M. Northampton. Two Northampton planes launched to conduct search one hundred fifty miles to the north.

11:21 A.M. Tennessee 2 list to port.

11:21 A.M. Tennessee To CINCPAC: Damage 30% to Tennessee, West Virginia sunk. Note: Correction West Virginia for California. Correction 00% instead of 30% for Tennessee.

11:25 A.M. Sumner fired four rounds 3" at plane crossing ahead from starboard, altitude 6,000 feet, no hits. Fired 50 caliber machine guns No. 1 and z

11:25 A.M. CPW 2 To VP 14 #1, VP 14 #3: STAY OUT.

11:30 A.M. Whitney received orders to remained at anchor.

11:30 A.M. Henley picked up captain and executive officer from Trever. No losses or damage experienced by Henley.

11:30 A.M. PATRON 24, CPW 2 to CPW 2, CTF 3: Eight men of war Lat. 2110, Long. 160 16, course 090 degrees.

11:30 A.M. Tennessee's bridge steering telegraph out (being repaired). Sending planes from Hickam Field.

11:32 A.M. Mugford observed horizontal bombers approaching from port (Jap.) t

11:33 A.M. St. Louis to COMDESRON 1: What is your position?

11:33 A.M. Sicard observed another horizontal bombing raid.

11:35 A.M. Sicard observed bombers withdrawing. No material damaged and no personnel casualties.

11:35 A.M. Sumner fired 11 rounds 3" at formation of five bombers crossing ahead from port no hits. Fired all machine guns.

11:35 A.M. CSD 43 To Comsubscofor: Point 21 54 Point 56 3L2.

11:35 A.M. Tennessee sighted two planes bearing Z70.

11:35 A.M. Breese picked up sound of submarine in same vicinity. Dropped two depth charges and oil slick with debris appeared. Second attack was made with four deep-set charges to make certain, but no additional results appeared. Meanwhile destroyers in vicinity dropped additional charges.

11:35 A.M. Northampton approximately fifteen miles west of Kauai. Section attacked by enemy single seat monoplane, engagement lasting about twenty minutes. Enemy plane made total of seven attacks diving from above or to the side of the scouting section. On all diving attacks presented and exceptionally good target as he squashed down toward the section. Apparent enemy speed 275 miles or better. Enemy plane broke out in smoke and departed. Search continued until completed.

11:35 A.M. Sumner fired eleven rounds 3" at formation of five bombers crossing ahead from port no hits. Fired all machine guns.

11:35 A.M. CSD 43 To Comsubscofor: Point 21 54 Point 56 3L2.

11:35 A.M. Tennessee sighted two planes bearing Z70 .

11:35 A.M. Mugford observed U. S. Navy planes taking off from Ford Island.

11:36 A.M. Tennessee observed light cruiser putting out to sea. Turning engines over to keep fire on water away from ship.

11:36 A.M. Mugford observed U. S. Navy planes taking off from Ford Island.

11:37 A.M. COMBATSHIP 3 To CTF 1: Minneapolis 2 DMs center southern boundary VICTOR ONE Course 105 speed 15/UKX CAB6.

11:39 A.M. CTF 8 To CINCPAC: TF 8 flying coalition?

11:39 A.M. CTF 9 To VP 24 Planes #1, #2, #4, #5, #11, CPW2: Search to 200 miles.

11:39 A.M. CTF 8 To CINCPAC: TF 8 flying colors bearing 184 distance 99 from Kaula Rock at 11:15 A.M.

11:40 A.M. Mugford observed Japanese planes on starboard beam.

11:40 A.M. RDO Wailupe To all stations this circuit: Guam attacked

11:40 A.M. DESBATFOR To CTF 8: Int posit desig zero george eight.

11:40 A.M. Northampton plane engaged enemy fighter. This was not known to Comtaskfor 8 until 8 December.

11:42 A.M. COM 14 To CINCPAC: Submarine due south Aloha Tower 4 miles has been bombed. Surface covered with oil slick.

11:43 A.M. COMBATFOR To COMBATSHIPS Prepare available battleship planes for search and report to subbase when ready and number. 2 California planes at Ford Island probably ready.

11:44 A.M. COMBASEFOR To COMINRON 2: Designate two DMs sweep approaches to Pearl magnetic mines.

11:45 A.M. COMCRUBATFOR To CINCPAC: Have no ships in sector 4.

11:46 A.M. Antares moored to B-5A Honolulu.

11:46 A.M. PATWING To Unknown: Enemy troops landing on north shore. Blue coveralls with red emblems.

11:50 A.M. COM 14 To CINCPAC: Parachutists are landing at Barber's Point.

11:52 A.M. CPW 1 To CINCPAC , CPW2: Three planes security patrol. Patrol fourteen are searching assigned sector. All planes have depth charges aboard.

11:53 A.M.3 COMCARDIV 1 To Cincpac: Saratoga ready depart San Diego at 9:00 A.M. tomorrow, Monday morning, escorting ships. So far as known have not been designated. Request instructions.

11:55 A.M. To ASP: All cruisers and destroyers depart Pearl as soon as practicable x report CTF 1 in Detroit.

11:56 A.M. Tennessee observed Army fortresses in the air. Believe enemy planes and submarines lying in channel.

11:59 A.M. Mugford. The end of period during which ship maintained 50 caliber and 5" fire.

12:00 P.M. Location of Forces 1200, 7 December 1941: T. F. 8 ENTERPRISE 21-:30 16s55- T. 1. 12 LEXINGTON. 23 50, 171-15- SUBDIV 43 (3 Submarines) 80 Miles East, coming ready; GUDGEON C-5, Ready; T. E. 1 and 2 less S in Pearl, T. F. 3 less 12, areas: Task F 3 rendezvousing with Minneapolis and 20Ms southern boundary VI Course 1:15.

12:00 P.M. Gwin To Comdesbatfor Reporting for duty with Lamson and Phelps: I am proceeding to South to locate and attack enemy carrier

12:00 P.M. Bobolink received orders from Combasefor to sweep Pearl Harbor with U.S.S. Turkey.

12:00 P.M. St. Louis To Comcruscofor: Reporting for duty with Lamson and Phelps. I am proceeding south to locate and attack enemy carrier.

12:01 P.M. COMPATWING To COMPATRON 24: Have search for assign sector 300 miles. Am returning.

12:02 P.M. CTF 8 To CINCPAC: Your 2100 refers Task Force 8 with thirteen ships X request all units be notified.

12:04 P.M. Gamble established sound contact with submarine and dropped three depth charges. Position bearing 16S T from Diamond Head light, distance 2.6 miles.

12:05 P.M. Comdesbatfor to Comdesflot ONE: About nine thirty witnessed Managhan sink enemy submarine by ramming and depth charges. Excellent piece of work.

12:05 P.M. SIGNAL TOWER About 9:30 A.M. witnessed Monagham sink enemy sub. by ramming and depth charges. Excellent piece of work. Believe Raleigh accounted for three planes.

12:05 P.M. Com 11 To Kennison: Submarine reported twenty miles bearing 23; from Pt. Loma investigate.

12:05 P.M. Com 14 All lights extinguished except control lights.

12:06 P.M. Mugford discontinued fueling. 115,000 gallons on board.

12:09 P.M. Mugford. Oil barge cleared starboard side.

12:09 P.M. COMBATSHIPS To CINCPAC: Design cast desig king baker jib.

12:09 P.M. COMBATSHIPS To Cruisers and Destroyers: Sortie in accordance until plan indicated.

12:10 P.M. Tennessee draft of ship (internal): Fwd. 34'6, Aft, 35'101/4- Mean 35'4 1/2". Enemy transport reported forty miles off Barber's Point. Parachute troops landing on Barber's Point (later proved false). After Battle Dressing Station send stretcher party to left gun, turret III, and remove casualties.

Three planes on starboard beam coming this way (do not know whether enemy or not). Said planes flying low; apparently, turning away. Organize a crew of about thirty men to relieve men of Turret IV who are fighting fire on water.

12:13 P.M. Solace to Com 14: Expedite your boat all tannic acid, tannic acid jelly, pecric acid, tetanus antitoxin, gas gangrene combined serum morphine sulphate, morphine syretts, sutures, needles, hypo needles and adhesive tape can be spared.

12:14 P.M. Mugford underway. Standing out in channel.

12:15 P.M. Helm rejoined Detroit. Ceased patrolling.

12:17 P.M. CTF 9 To PW 21,23,19: Search to three hundred miles.

12:21 P.M. RDO Wailupe to all stations: Nine unidentified aircraft over Guam.

12:16 P.M. SIGNAL TOWER. These ships have cleared Pearl Harbor Channel: Dale, Hanley, Patterson, Phoenix, Wasmuth, Ramsey, St. Louis, Detroit, Montgomery, Worden, Cummings.

12:19 P.M. Combatships To Com 14 Serious oil fire alongside West Virginia. Tennessee and Maryland send fire boats.

12:23 P.M. CTF 8 To CINCPAC: 21 VSB from Enterprise should have landed Ford Island about 8:30 A.M. Request information.

12:23 P.M. RDO Wailupe To ASP: Air alarm standby.

12:26 P.M. Bobolink moored alongside coal dock to take wire aboard.

12:23 P.M. CINCPAC To ASP Hawaiian Area: If NPM fox goes out guard harbor circuit.

12:28 P.M. Combat ships To CINCPAC: Pennsylvania dive bomb hit starboard side frame 86 drydock now flooded.

Maryland magazines flooded.

Tennessee fire in wardroom country.

Oklahoma capsized.

West Virginia sunk but upright.

California down by the head and heavy list to port probably on bottom.

Arizona sunk.

Nevada beached off Hospital Point. Unknown CPW 2 To VP 23: Search to 200 miles any instructions.

12:29 P.M. SIGNAL TOWER. Thornton is underway and standing up.

12:30 P.M. Tennessee secure. All fresh water, except galley and drinking.

12:30 P.M. Curtiss to incpac. Unable to sortie because of damage.

12:30 P.M. Mugford observed Japanese plane crashed on beach of Hickam Field. (Note: It is believed the ship observed this at this time (wreckage), not that the crash occurred at this time.

12:30 P.M. While Gamble conducting depth charge attack off Diamond Head, received three dispatches from Cinc addressed to ASP.

Ships ordered to attack transports reported four miles off Barber's Point. All vessels having departed Pearl Harbor organized as Task Force ONE to report to CTF 8 clearing harbor and to report position, composition, and speed.

Gamble continued with depth charge attack until contact was lost then proceeded to Barber's Point where no transports were found Continued westward.

12:32 P.M. CINCPAC To ASP: Enemy transports reported four miles off Barbers Point. Attack.

12:35 P.M. CTF 12 To CTF 3 & 8: Cancel Midway Marine flight.

12:35 P.M. CTF 12 To CINCPAC: Is Midway flight canceled.

12:35 P.M. Mugford passed entrance to channel. Four 50 cal. and four 5"/38 cal guns during the entire period 8:09 A.M. to 11:59 A.M. whenever any planes came within range and bearing maintained fire.

12:35 P.M. COMBAT SHIPS To Combatfor: Combat ship in Maryland.

12:35 P.M. Raleigh To CINCPAC: Two fire rooms and engine room and stern compartment flooded. Damage under control at present. Unable to get underway.

12:40 P.M. MU" HE SARA HAHO On 4780 BRG 186 (Believed Submarine).

12:44 P.M. Plane 12 VP 23 Two CPW2: Approaching 300 yards able to search more gas 400 25 I request instructions.

12:45 P.M. Tennessee. Planes on port bow (do not know whether enemy or not).

12:46 P.M. California sinking fast, stern underwater. Close all topside hatches, as turrets will be fired. (Did not). Gun four port reported Hoist #22, 5"/51, in B-510 was damaged. Power can be sent up but is slowed. Draft of ship, FORWARD: 34'9". Magazine temperature of Turret I-84 .

12:46 P.M. WP OFF. 14ND High altitude bombing attack coming in over Diamond Head. Unknown CINCPAC To RDO San Diego: Receive me on 26.1, transmit on 30.6 (cable to Navy radio San Diego) Via Globe.

12:47 P.M. Curtiss To CPW2: All of our transmitters are out.

12:47 P.M. Combat ships To Colorado: If vessels are no longer in service will furnish men and officers to ships in service to man complete Anti-Aircraft batteries for continuous watch.

12:48 P.M. Combasefor To COMINRON TWO: Designate two Destroyer Minesweepers sweep approach to Pearl magnetic mines.

12:55 P.M. U.S.S. Gamble proceeded on course 270T at 20 knots to join friendly forces upon receipt of orders from CINCPAC.

12:56 P.M. MTB SQUAD Out guarding 3445 voice sqdn. Comdrs. PT 20 PT 22, PT 23, PT 24 At dock guarding 3445 voice PT 21. On dock at crane no power PT 26, PT 28. Aboard RAMAPO underway (Patrol boats) PT 27, PT 29, PT 30, PT 42.

12:58 P.M. Com 14 Four Japanese transports off Barbers Point.

1:00 P.M. St. Louis to Comdesbatfor: St. Louis, Blue, Lamson, Phelps position Latitude 20.51 Long 158, course 275, speed 25K. Unknown Cincpac To CTF 8: Your 2208 Only nine arrived.

1:00 P.M. Kanure appears to be O.T.C. on 6581 BRG. 183.

1:00 P.M. Siso on 7033 BRG 1671/2.

1:00 P.M. Kaso Seems to be Task Force Commander.

1:00 P.M. Kanure is probably Commander in the Air.

1:00 P.M. Raleigh reports Navy tugs U.S.S. Sunnadin (AT-28) and Avocet came alongside and furnished light and power. One torpedo ran between bow of Raleigh and stern of Detroit, and apparently sank in shallow water at Ford Island without exploding.

The following planes were destroyed, in which it is considered the Raleigh contributed:

1. Bomber flying over stern starboard to port crashed on deck of Curtiss.

2. Plane new over bow from starboard to port and crashed near Pearl City.

3. Plane flying north on our starboard beam crashed in water between Dobbin and Baltimore.

4. Plane off our stern flying over Air Station was hit by 3" shell and blown to pieces in air.

5. Plane flying across our stern had tail blown off and fell Over Pearl City. 1300 Comdesbatfor own destroyers reports no enemy vessels off Barbers Point.

1:00 P.M. CTF 1 joined Detroit course 210 n speed 18 from point 51. (Action to St. Louis)

1:00 P.M. Ramsay observed Japanese ship four miles from Barbers Point Two sampans further out. Parachute troops landing on North Shore. (Reported by VJ plane.)

1:01 P.M. CPW 2 Search sector 220 to 230. Return (Action to 12-VP-23) Unknown Comtrainron 8. Antares docked pier five affirm, Honolulu. Struck by several machine gun bullets but no damage to material or personnel.

1:02 P.M.1302 Cincpac To CTF 8: Radio bearings indicate Akagi bearing 183 from Pearl another unit bearing 167.

1:03 P.M. CPW 2 To COMSCORON 6: Reported Jap rendezvous 223 ninety miles from Ford Island. Search to two hundred miles sector 235 to 215.

1:05 P.M. NAS Kaneohe captured enemy chart has marked positions bearing 223 distant ninety miles from Pearl Harbor.

1:09 P.M. Signal Tower Detroit and Phoenix are near Barbers Point. Signal Tower sees no transports.

1:10 P.M. Combasefor To comtrainron 6; Com 14, COMINRON 2: Sweep channel from East Loch to entrance magnetic and Moored mines.

1:12 P.M. Hulbert Army reports that four enemy transports off Barbers Point.

1:12 P.M. ST. Louis. Am proceeding with three destroyers to attack Barbers Point Speed two five position lat. 21-57 long 150-03.

1:13 P.M. Combatships To NAS Pearl: for Captain Bode of U.S.S. California urgently needs Anti-Aircraft ammunition.

1:17 P.M. Radio communicatios Wailupe Signals intercepted and bearing true north believed to be enemy carrier by character of transmission.

1:19 P.M. U.S.S. Frank Cable (AS-40) a Submarine Tender By phone: Enemy sampan (a flat bottomed wooden Chinese boat) about to land at Naval ammunition Depot. Frank reports enemy landing party off shore

Nanakul. Friendly planes firing at them.

Frank. Op-1 Southeast enemy and friendly planes in dogfight.

1:22 P.M. Enemy naval attack coming in towards Barbers Point. Present position nine miles.

1:22 P.M. Opnav To Mardet Tientsin. Com 15, Mardet AM Emb, Peiping Astnavatt Shanghai, Radio communications Wake, Navatt Chungking, Johnston Island, Radio communications, Guam, Palmyra, Com 16, Rdo Tutuila.

Hopkins: This confirms air raid by Japan on Oahu at 6:00 P.M. today followed by declaration of war by Japan against US and Great Britain.

1:23 P.M. Helena To Comcrubatfor: Due to contamination of feed water cannot maintain underway status longer than eight hours. During this time speed limited to ten knots. Ready this condition on one hour notice F power for fire control limited to two diesel generators. View condition and to effect repairs. Recommend letting fires under all boilers die out.

1:24 P.M. CTF 8: UPSN Junction Task Force One and Eight. Propose send Crudiv Five to Pearl for fuel.

1:28 P.M. Minneapolis. Your 072234 (CincPacs) complying. Ref. # 12-299 Use plane to search sector 135 to 180 distance 154 miles from Pearl. ----

CINCPAC To CTF 8: Detroit, Phoenix, St. Louis, New Orleans fourteen destroyers and four minelayers have sortied and are proceeding to join you.

Also, Minneapolis and four minelayers ordered to join from operating areas send ships to Pearl for fuel.

1:30 P.M. Bobolink's orders to sweep channel changed to sweeping approaches to Pearl Harbor and Honolulu Harbor. Arriving off Pearl it appeared all ships there were engaged in sweeping.

1:30 P.M. Reports 7632 kcs (M) following calls: Sime; Sisc: Dascho: Suremo, Samore. Sends following type of 095.45 086.42 1337 Bearing OD SISC 170 85 1341 Bearing on Samore 165 1344 Reports following mag KISC to Sime Nr. 1 Sime 354. 56 1345 Reports SOSC Good bearing 7632 (M) 337.

1:31 P.M. CTF 1 To CINCPAC: Task Force ONE: proceeding off Barbers Point Notify Army.

1:33 P.M. CPW 1 To CPW 2: Request instructions for dawn patrol upon their re- turn. 1337 CTF 3 To CTF 2: My force Indianapolis and

5 Destroyer Mine sweeps. Indianapolis proceeding from Johnston Island course 054 speed 25. Dog Mike Sail directed proceed Pearl for fuel and rejoin later.

1:40 P.M. Tennessee. Plane coming in on starboard beam. (Proved to be friendly).

1:45 P.M. CTF 8 launched 9 VSB's to cover sector 110-200T to 175 miles. One of latter reported contact with surface forces believed enemy including a carrier in position Latitude 20-32 Long 158-16 and cruiser Latitude 20-32 Long 158-40. Scout reported being attacked by VF's. No further radio con- tact established with scout. U.S.S. Scout (DE-214) a Destroyer Escort ship, landed later at Kaneohe, reports believed to have been in error.

1:48 P.M. Vireo. Received orders to report to Combasefor thence to West Loch to bring up 5", 3" and .50 M. G. ammunition for California.

1:51 P.M. Reports SISC calling Samore. S5 bearing 337. Very loud signal

1:53 P.M. Reports bearing Samemu bearing 337. Following bearings: 7632 kcs (M) 0036-Susu S5 340-7632 (M) 0040 Sime 336 Following bearings: 7632 (M) 005-bearing Sisc 338 S.5 7050 (M) 0055 bearing Sisc 33S.5 S.5 1410 Kanure says at 12:35 P.M. (local time) "I HAVE FUEL FOR 10 MINUTES"

Kanure at 12:40 P.M. "I WILL FLY AS LONG AS I HAVE FUEL." Someone on 7033 at 12:47 P.M. said "HAVE NOT BE OPPOSED,"

Same frequency believed to be Sinire from Sisc at 12:50 P.M. "WHAT IS YOUR COURSE".

RUS18 and YUNE8 believed to be Commander Carrier SUT12 believed to be a Carrier.

Sisore is either another Commander in the Air or Commander Transport Group 1.

Siso is boss of Sisore. No further bearings of radio intelligence of the Striking Force until following day of 8 December 1941.

2:12 P.M. Gamble sighted sampan bearing 32 T.

2:15 P.M. Tennessee Set condition ZED from Turret III, second deck, aft. Repair I, Unit 2, leading out fire hose to distribute water on West Virginia. Received report that one of our destroyers sank jap submarine.

2:26 P.M. Bobolink passed sweep wire to Turkey and commenced sweeping off Honolulu Harbor.

2:35 P.M. Gamble slowed to investigate but did not search, sampan position, approximately four miles south of Barbers Point.

TRANSMISSION:

2:50 P.M. Sime 010.01 I HA NKIARIYA ANSWER: 2 HA NKIARI BEARINGS Saremu 338 S.4 on 7632 kcs (M) 1410 Wasmuth rigs twin ship moored mine sweep with USS Zane, 400 fathoms of wire between ships, depressors at 5 fathoms, no floats.

2:55 P.M. Vireo. While waiting for arrival of ammunition, towed ammunition lighter with 14" powder away from dock to decrease menace to explosion. Delivered ammunition to Argonne.

3:47 P.M. Entered Pearl Harbor entrance channel and sweep up channel to gate vessel, where wire parted.

4:20 P.M. Anchored off Coal Dock and retrieved sweep gear.

4:20 P.M. Underway.

4:35 P.M. The Captain returned aboard, Lieutenant Commander Agnew, USN, left and joined Trever. Returned off harbor entrance and resumed patrol in company with Mindiv 4.

3:00 P.M. TENNESSEE Report states that Wake Island had been bombed by 30 bombers. Ens. Kable still alive, Hudgell dead: also, Miller and Adams. [96] Midway 4:00 P.M. Via commercial Cable."on 7073 SISO 2-16 Fair Sime 245 Poor NAS Midway." Plane language : SASO V SAREMI #3 A FU"KUMA YORI 150 to "30 MAIRU NEN 200 1115 .

3:05 P.M. Dewey underway and standing out of harbor.

3:50 P.M. Bobolink. Received orders from Commander Base Force to report 1010 dock immediately. 1

3:51 P.M. 551 Tennessee Repair 4 All outboard voids normal. All soundings nor- mal.

Received report that Pennsylvania had been hit while in drydock. No. 2 machine gun repaired and in commission again.

3:52 P.M. CTF 12 given orders by CTF 8 to intercept and destroy possible enemy carriers operating south coast of Oahu. It was assumed after attacks enemy carriers would withdraw via Jaluit.

3:58 P.M. Gamble sighted bomb off port bow.

4:28 P.M. Tennessee. Open up wardroom country and sleepy hollow. Fire on West Virginia seems to be under control. Repair I cut off # 32 vent system: smoke coming down.

4:30 P.M. Task Force ONE just ordered by CTF 8 proceed and attack.

4:31 P.M. Gamble reports submarine surfaced.

4:32 P.M. Gamble fired one shot 4" gun and missed, short and to the left. Submarine displayed U. S. colors and ceased firing. Submarine submerged and fired recognition red smoke bomb.

4:40 P.M. Bobolink. While off dock 1010 received orders to assist Nevada. Orders changed to go alongside California.

4:42 P.M. Attack group of 16 VF, 18 VTB's and 4 VSB smokers launched by Comtaskforce EIGHT with no results. (VTB planes armed with torpedoes recovered after dark.) Six VF planes proceeded Pearl mistaken for unfriendly and four shot down.

4:47 P.M. Gamble proceeded west.

4:47 P.M. Tennessee told forward battle dressing station to send doctor and stretcher party to West Virginia bridge to get Captain. Ship astern (Arizona) blew up. Two planes bearing 350.

4:55 P.M. Whitney reports Case left from alongside.

4:59 P.M. Tennessee engines ahead 1/3. Repairs 2 and 4; send two rescue breathers each, and spare oxygen bottles to starboard side of West Virginia quarterdeck.

5:03 P.M. Tennessee, Word received to stop main engines. Delivered six gas masks to West Virginia.

5:05 P.M. Whitney reports Tucker left from alongside.

5:30 P.M. Bobolink moored alongside Widgeon next to California for salvage purposes.

5:32 P.M. Gamble sighted Enterprise and exchanged calls. Instructed by Commander Aircraft. Battle Force to join Enterprise.

5:36 P.M. Comairbatfor ordered Gamble to join that vessel as part of AS Screen.

5:40 P.M. Bobolink commenced pumping to continue through the night.

5:41 P.M. Gamble joined Enterprise and took station as third ship with two other plane guard destroyers.

5:55 P.M. Pelias moored at Berths S-11 and 12, Submarine Base, reports first attack was indicated by sound of machine gun fire directed at single engine Jap torpedo plane flying low over ship's bow. The plane launched a torpedo at Arizona which soon later burst into flames.

5:55 P.M. Tennessee. Plane bearing 345. Plane signaled with red light; did not understand meaning of signal.

6:00 P.M. Pennsylvania reports complete replacement of ammunition effected.

6:23 P.M. Tennessee observed plane bearing about 300.

6:30 P.M. Tennessee. Plane on port beam; running lights on.

6:33 P.M. Tennessee. Plane bearing about 345 (Running lights on; believed friendly).

6:37 P.M. Tennessee. Plane coming in from dead ahead; bright lights on it.

6:38 P.M. Tennessee. Plane bearing about 245.

6:55 P.M. Tennessee AND U.S.S. Enterprise (CV-6) Aircraft Carrier's planes approaching Oahu.

7:53 P.M. Tennessee. Plane bearing from dead ahead; running lights burning.

9:00 P.M. Tennessee. Word passed over loudspeaker "All men having hammocks in port hammock nettings remove them and stow same inboard."

9:00 P.M. Tracy reports friendly planes with running lights were by Anti-Aircraft batteries, but Tracy did not fire.

9:00 P.M. Tracy moored alongside California and commenced salvage work.

9:00 P.M. Sicard observed three lighted planes, altitude five thousand approaching Ford Island from South. New Orleans challenged without success and opened fired. Other ships followed too.

Sicard checked fire considering planes were friendly. Other ships continued firing.

9:10 P.M. Vireo observed Anti-Aircraft fire opened and planes shot down. Aviator fell astern of Vireo, was rescued, and identified from Enterprise. Dispatch was sent to inform control that Enterprise planes were in air. At this point the battle was over.

The aftermath of the Pearl Harbor Battle. Over twenty American Ships were damaged or destroyed, three hundred U.S. aircrafts were damaged. A total of 2,400 Americans died including civilians and over 1,000 people were wounded. 1,177 men died on the U.S.S. Arizona.

THE ACT OF WAR TIMELINE

On December 6, 1941, at 2200 hours (10 P.M.) the U.S.S. Condor (AMC-14), a United States (U.S.) Navy Coastal minesweeper crew, was patrolling in grid style maneuvers. They were a mile and a half from the entrance to the Pearl Harbor channel. They were on high alert due to an incident reported.

On December 5th, two officers stationed on board the battleship U.S.S. Nevada (BB-36) spotted what appeared to be a periscope from a submarine. We had no submarines active in that area. Due to this, the U.S. Navy was on alert.

At about 2330 hours (11:30 P.M.), I was awakened by my shipmate, Jim Brown II, so I could stand my lookout watch. He was a deck seaman. He always woke me up in time to eat before reporting for my lookout watch duty. We called the meals sea rats, short for sea rations. The cooks kept us fed. The on-coming and off-going watch personnel were allowed a hot meal.

I made it down to the ship's Galley in time for sloppy joes and potato chips with a big cup of Joe (coffee) black and strong. I also drank a cup of bug juice which is what we called cherry flavored Kool-Aid type beverage.

At 2345 (11:45), I reported to the ship's forecastle, the forward part of the ship, to relieve my shipmate, Dean Smith (Smitty). He passed on the information that it was quiet and boring. We always reported for our watch fifteen minutes before the hour. We used big powerful binoculars which were Mark I Model 2 made by Bausch & Lomb. They were 7X50 which means that they have 7X magnification and the lenses are 50mm in diameter. We also had a head set communication device, used to talk with the pilot house.

It was around 0230 hours (2:30 A.M.) on the early morning of Sunday, December 7, 1941. Chief Petty Officer Bill Jones who was a Boatswain's mate. (Boatswain's mates take care of the Ship's maintenance, cleaning, painting) He was making his rounds and checking on the watch. He brought me some fresh hot coffee in a big metal thermos. He told me a couple of funny sea stories then moved on to the next man on watch. There were three people on lookout. One man in the pilot house, one on the Bow (Front) and the Stern (Rear) and the forecastle where I was posted.

I was also a certified Expert Lookout. I had above-average eyesight. Normal eyesight is 20/20 and mine is 20/10. I remember it was a little chilly that morning with a northeast wind at eleven miles per hour and about forty-eight degrees Fahrenheit. I had my peacoat on and it kept me warm.

At approximately 0342 hours (3:42 A.M.) The Officer of the Deck on duty in the Pilot house, Ensign McCloy, noticed a disturbance in the water bearing 260 degrees about twenty yards out on the port (left) side of the ship. We had good visibility due to the reflection of the moon light. He saw what looked like a periscope from a submarine. I looked and confirmed the contact. Navy Quartermaster Ray Chavez was on duty in the Pilot house. Ray looked hard at this contact breaking the water, near the entrance to Pearl Harbor, through binoculars and agreed that it was a periscope. There were no U.S. Navy submarines on duty in that area. This had to be an enemy submarine. This was a serious situation at hand.

At 0357 hours (3:57 A.M.), the Condor sent a message to U.S.S. Ward (DD-139), a Navy Destroyer using a Yardarm blinker which is a signal device used to communicate from ship to ship by using a series of red-light messages using a special code. Our message read "Sighted submarine on westerly course, speed 9 knots." The U.S.S. Ward was cruising at fifteen knots and patrolling two-mile grid squares just off the Pearl Harbor entrance.

The Captain, William Woodward Outerbridge, of the Ward was well aware of the critical relationship between the United States and Japan. The Captain ordered, "General Quarters, General Quarters! Man your battle stations!"

He then asked the Condor to report the contact's (submarine's) course and speed. The Condor's response was "last sighting at 0350 hours (3:50 A.M.) with the submarine heading towards the entrance to Pearl Harbor." The Ward started using sonar to search for submarine in the area, which resulted in negative results.

At 0435 h ours (4:35 A.M.) General Quarters were secured. The U.S.S. Antares (AKS-3) which was a stores and supply ship was carrying a light load in tow, moving slowly towards Pearl Harbor. Her Captain, Commander Lawrence C. Grannis, was waiting for a U.S. Navy tugboat and a harbor pilot to help navigate clear passage through the straits in the channel. The channel was extremely rocky and dangerous in certain spots in the harbor entrance. This would help them deliver her safe and sound to her berth in Pearl Harbor.

At 0630 hours (6:30 A.M.), Commander Grannis spotted an object about fifteen hundred yards off the starboard side. This object didn't look like any submarine that he had seen before. The submarine's conning tower was above the water's surface which made it easier to identify it as a submarine. It appeared to be having depth control problems.

The Ward was contacted about the sighting at 0640 h ours (6:40 A.M.) and the Ward sounded General Quarters once again. The order was given to go all engines on full speed ahead towards the direction of the submarine. The Ward opened fire towards the contact and her first shot missed the target. She fired again and the second shot hit at the waterline. The conning tower of the submarine sunk below.

Those shots fired by the Destroyer U.S.S. Ward (DD-139) are known to be the first shots at Pearl Harbor fired against the Japanese.

The Ward the dropped a depth charge set at a depth of one hundred feet, near the sinking submarine.

The Captain of the Ward immediately notified the 14th Naval District Watch Officer to report the incident. He reported, "We have dropped depth charges upon a submarine operating in the Defensive Sea Area." The Captain wanted to be more complete, so he sent a second message which was "We have attacked, fired upon, and dropped depth charges upon a submarine operating in the Defensive Sea Area. "

A Bishop Point radio station logged in this message at 0653 hours (6:53 A.M.) This was just two hours and two minutes before the Pearl Harbor attack. The U.S. Coast Guard Cutter Tiger (WSC-152), a submarine chaser, was on duty patrolling in an area between Barbers Point and Diamond Head located in Mamalo Bay. Her assigned patrol area was just south where the Ward was located.

At 0400 hours (4:00 A.M.) the Tiger's Midwatch had just completed the changing of the watch when we heard the news that the Ward had sunk an enemy submarine in the Harbor area. As the Tiger arrived near the south shoreline, she begun to track any submarine activity. The first contact was thought to be a whale but was quickly dismissed when motor noises were heard. It was most definitely a submarine. It was headed straight towards the entrance to Pearl Harbor.

The Tiger lost contact with the submarine but continued towards the harbor. Just as she entered the harbor the Japanese sneak air attack was just starting. The Tiger turned and headed full speed out of the harbor. The Tiger was now a target and did receive some damage as she was being fired upon.

U.S.S. Ward

U.S.S. Condor

THE DAY OF INFAMY SPEECHBY:

FRANKLIN D. ROOSEVELT

Mr. Vice President, and Mr. Speaker, and Members of the Senate and House of Representatives:

Yesterday, December 7, 1941, a date which will live in infamy, the United States of America was suddenly and deliberately attacked by naval and air forces of the Empire of Japan.

The United States was at peace with that Nation and, at the solicitation of Japan, was still in conversation with its Government and its Emperor looking toward the maintenance of peace in the Pacific.

Indeed, one hour after Japanese air squadrons had commenced bombing in the American Island of Oahu, the Japanese Ambassador to the United States and his colleague delivered to our Secretary of State a formal reply to a recent American message. And while this reply stated that it seemed useless to continue the existing diplomatic negotiations, it contained no threat or hint of war or of armed attack.

It will be recorded that the distance of Hawaii from Japan makes it obvious that the attack was deliberately planned many days or even weeks ago.

During the intervening time, the Japanese Government has deliberately sought to deceive the United States by false statements and expressions of hope for continued peace.

The attack yesterday on the Hawaiian Islands has caused severe damage to American naval and military forces. I regret to tell you that very many American lives have been lost. In addition, American ships have been reported torpedoed on the high seas between San Francisco and Honolulu.

The President requests War Declaration. Yesterday the Japanese government also launched an attack against Malaya. Last night, Japanese forces attacked Hong Kong. Last night Japanese forces attacked Guam. Last night Japanese forces attacked the Philippine Islands. Last night the Japanese attacked Wake Island. And this morning, the Japanese attacked Midway Island. Japan has, therefore, undertaken a surprise offensive extending throughout the Pacific area.

The facts of yesterday and today speak for themselves. The people of the United States have already formed their opinions and well understand the implications to the very life and safety of our Nation. As Commander in Chief of the Army and Navy, I have directed that all measures be taken for our defense. But always will our whole Nation remember the character of the onslaught against us.

STORIES FROM PEARL HARBOR SURVIVORS

CHIEF YEOMAN (YNC)

Kenneth Capps

This is a survivor's story as told by Barbara Wayt, daughter of Chief Yeoman (YNC) Kenneth Capps. Kenneth Capps told his daughter, Barbara Wayt, about his military service and the attack on Pearl Harbor.

I joined the United States Navy around 1939 and I attended Boot Camp (Basic Training) at Great Lakes, Illinois.

After graduating from Boot Camp, I was off to Meridian, Mississippi to complete my "A" school for technical, administrative, and clerical training for the rate (job) of yeoman. My training lasted for approximately seven weeks.

To be considered for the rate of Yeoman, a person has to have good communication skills with administration and clerical work as their main job. They are responsible for all the paperwork. One of the main jobs in the Navy for a Yeoman is to pass a typing test.

I was then off to the fleet and was stationed on board the battleship U.S.S California (BB-44). The California was the second of two Tennessee class battleships built for the U.S. Navy. Her keel was laid on October 25, 1916. She was built at the Mare Island naval shipyard in Vallejo, California and was officially commissioned on August 10,1921.

The U.S.S. California was launched on November 20, 1919. She joined the Pacific Fleet after her sea trails. The U.S.S. California was outfitted with a battery of twelve 14" (356 mm) guns in four three-gun turrets. The California was the flag ship of the battle group Pacific Fleet and completed several gun firing exercises.

On Saturday, December 6, 1941, I remember being on board ship busy shining my dress shoes and belt buckle. I wanted to be finished and squared away with getting my uniform all ready. We were scheduled to have a personnel uniform inspection by Admiral Husband Edward Kimmel on Monday, December 8, 1941.

Afterwards, I made my way to the chow line for supper. I remember we had fried chicken with spuds and gravy and green peas. We had peach cobbler with ice cream for dessert.

I was studying for my second-class petty officer exam. I took a quick shower then laid in my rack and listened to some Hawaiian music being transmitted on Hawaii's radio station. KGU-AM was a commercial radio station that first hit air waves on May 11, 1922, and was located in Honolulu, Hawaii.

I tuned into a local station on my new small portable radio model 802. I listened for a while then I shut it off to save battery power. I got off to sleep just prior to taps. Sunday morning Reveille was sounded at 0600 hours (6 a.m.). I went off to the head (bathroom) splashed water in my face and brushed my teeth. Then it was off to the chow line.

I met up with my shipmate, Wayne Shelnutt. We got our chow which consisted of scrambled eggs, bacon and fried taters, and toast. We were also served big cups of milk and coffee. I remembered that we had finished eating and were drinking our coffee when we realized we were under attack.

The California was hit both forward and aft by two Japanese torpedoes around 0755 hours (7:55 a. m.) The ship called out, "General quarters, general quarters! Man your battle stations!" on the loudspeaker.

I was one deck below the main deck and was going up a ladder on the way to the main deck. My best friend was just behind me just starting up the ladder way when a bomb hit our ship. My friend did not make it. He was killed by the bomb. This was the most difficult memory of Pearl Harbor and always so painful to even talk about it.

We started to take on water from the torpedo hits. The bomb took out the ship's electrical system, therefore, we were unable to use our pumps to pump out all the water we were taking on. We had full steam and had plans of getting underway.

Due to a massive amount of burning oil that was drifting towards us and was getting too close for comfort coming from battleship row, we thought it would set our ship on fire.

The officer of the deck ordered all of us to abandon ship. I remember the "Jap" planes were flying so low you could see their faces as they dropped bombs and torpedoes. We had to climb over our dead crew mates to be able to jump over the side of the rolling ship. I helped other shipmates to the shore of Ford Island by swimming under the flames from the oil and fuel burning on top of the water.

The worst part was the next day, Monday, December 8, 1941. We had to take bags and pick up body parts that had washed up on the shore for burial. It was a dirty job, and we all were filthy because of the oil in the water and on the bodies. There was no food or drinks available for us.

A total of one hundred three crew members were killed and sixty-one were wounded. The circumstances and remains of a total of twenty sailors from battleship California remain unresolved.

After Pearl Harbor, I served on the Admiral's flag ship for Rear Admiral Royal Ingersoll who took over command of the U.S.S. Augusta (CA-31). She was a Northampton-class heavy cruiser named after Augusta, Georgia. She also became a presidential flag ship with President Franklin D. Roosevelt and Harry S. Truman in wartime conditions.

I served most of the rest of the war on the U.S.S. Augusta and served during several campaigns including Operation Torch from November 8, 1942, to November 16,1942. Operation Torch was an allied invasion of French North Africa during the second world war.

I also served on the campaign known as Operation Overlord from June 6, 1944, to August 30, 1944.

In 1946, after the war, I was stationed on Guam Island. Guam is an island located in Micronesia in the western pacific. It is unique due to the tropical beaches and Chamorro villages and the ancient latte-stone pillars. Guam is a United States island territory and is a military installation for the U.S. Navy in Santa Rita and Anderson air force base in Yigo. Also, the Guam army national guard was stationed there. I was stationed there until 1948.

During the Korean war, I was assigned to the U.S.S. Coral Sea (CVA-43). She was a midway-class aircraft carrier and was the third ship of the United States Navy to be named for the battle of the Coral Sea. Her nickname was "Ageless Warrior."

Her keel was laid down on July 10, 1944. She was launched on April 2, 1946, and commissioned on October 1,1947 with Captain A.P. Storrs, III in command. While I was serving on the Coral Sea, the ship also made a Mediterranean cruise.

Chief Yeoman (YNC) Kenneth Capps retired from the United States Navy in 1956 after serving twenty years.

Thank you for your service, Sir. Much respect!

LONNIE DAVID COOK

1920 – 2019

Author's note from Shannon Cooper:

I had the honor and privilege of knowing Lonnie Cook personally. I met Lonnie back in 2012 when I served as the Chaplain for Veterans of Foreign Wars (VFW) Post 1189 in Okmulgee, Oklahoma. Our Post, along with the Okmulgee Elks Lodge, was having a luncheon to honor Lonnie Cook. There were other invited guests, but Lonnie and his wife, Marietta, were the guests of honor.

I invited my granddaughter, Cadence Cooper who was still very young at that time. I wanted her to have the experience of being with our veterans and seeing how we honored them.

We had a nice lunch where I gave the benediction. I also made and decorated a full sheet cake with the image of the U.S.S. Arizona on it. Additionally, I did an oil painting of the U.S.S. Arizona and personally presented it to Lonnie.

After the luncheon, all the VFW members returned to the Post. Lonnie introduced me to his wife, and we all had cake and coffee. She was really a nice lady.

I also remember playing several games of pool with Lonnie. That's when I first heard Lonnie's story of survival of Pearl Harbor for the first time. It is an incredible personal account of what he and his shipmates experienced together.

I remember telling Lonnie that he and I had a couple of things in common. He said, "Oh, yeah? What's that?" I told him that we were both battleship sailors. He served where the World War II started and I served on the ship, the U.S.S. Missouri, where World II ended on board the decks on September 2, 1945.

I kept up with him and his wife and visited both of them several times in Morris, Oklahoma.

I also ran into him often at the VA Hospital in Muskogee, Oklahoma.

In 2016, my granddaughter, Cadence, was given an assignment for her History class project. This assignment to interview and American hero was given to the students prior to Veterans Day in 2016.

At first, she approached me and wanted to interview me. I was touched and very humbly declined as I explained to her that I was no hero. However, I did tell her that I knew of an American hero who she might be able to interview.

I phoned my shipmate Lonnie and told him about the assignment and that my granddaughter would love to speak with him. Cadence talked to him over the phone and explained her school assignment. Lonnie graciously agreed to a one-on-one interview with her.

I planned a spaghetti dinner for Lonnie and his wife and invited Cadence to spend the weekend at our house. The dinner was a complete success.

After dinner, we all went to the living room where Cadence had a cassette recorder set up to record the interview which Lonnie had agreed would be fine with him. She asked him a few questions to insure she got his story correct and had his permission to tell his story.

This is Lonnie's story as told by Lonnie Cook himself.

MS2 Shannon R. Cooper, U.S.N.R.

I joined the United States Navy on April 3,1940. As soon as I joined, I traveled by train to Little Rock, Arkansas to be sworn in. Then I was off to boot camp in San Diego, California Recruit Training Center.

After boot camp in June 1940, I went through Seamanship training. Then off to my first fleet assignment which was the USS Arizona BB-39. I got a ride from San Diego to Pearl Harbor, Hawaii on board the USS Enterprise (CV-6) which is a big E Aircraft carrier. It was the biggest ship I had ever seen.

It took a week to arrive to Pearl Harbor. I reported for duty on board the Arizona and was assigned to the Third Division. My work area was located on the starboard (right side) quarter deck of the ship and gun turret number three.

I was assigned to the Deck Force, and I had to get up early in the mornings to Holystone the Teak wood decks. Holystone is a soft and brittle sandstone used by the Navy for scrubbing and whitening the wooden deck of the ships. I had to wash it down and also polish the brass. There was a lot of brass on a battleship.

We were in a compartment located just forward of the Quarter deck. This where we slept and ate. We slept on hammocks. It was so hot at night that we would just lay there and sweat. In the morning, we got up and folded our hammocks up, put it in the netting even though it would still be wet from sweat from the night before.

While in high school, I had taken a typing class because it was an easy class. Since I had knew how to type, I was able to move up and work in the Gunnery office. This was a step up from being a deck hand.

A few weeks after reporting on board the Arizona, we got underway and departed Pearl Harbor to set off to the seas in the south Pacific on a Western Pacific (West Pac) cruise.

Our first port of call was Subic Bay in the Philippine Islands. We had a crazy time in Subic. The food was really good. The one thing I remember about the Philippines is that it was really humid there. Our clothes just stuck to us. They used fans everywhere. We left Subic Bay and went back out to sea.

We crossed the Equator and went through Shellback initiation. We transitioned from being a Pollywog to becoming a Shellback. It's a rite of passage and a tradition in the Navy dating back at least four hundred years. It observes a mariner's transformation from slimy Pollywog, a seaman who has not crossed the Equator, to a trusty Shellback. A Shellback is also called a Son or Daughter of Neptune. It was a way for sailors to be tested for their seaworthiness. We did a lot of battle drills where we did maneuvers and shoot off the big guns.

In October 1940, we headed back stateside to Bremerton, Washington Naval Shipyards. We were in dry docks. I remember they scrapped off a lot of barnacles off the bottom of the ship. We were there for three months, then back to our home port of Pearl Harbor.

In October 1941, we went back out to sea where we had a rendezvous and battle training maneuvers with the USS Oklahoma (BB-37). While engaged in battle training exercises, there was a heavy rainstorm and visibility was at a minimum. On October 22, 1941, the Oklahoma was making a starboard turn as part of the maneuvers and collided with the Arizona and hit us. This caused severe damage to the side of the ship about the size of a box car.

The Arizona limped back to Pearl Harbor and directly went into the shipyard dry docks for a quick repair. We were not supposed to be there, but due to casualties, we were delayed going back to Bremerton shipyard.

I was twenty-one years old and went out on liberty on Saturday night in Honolulu. I had a great time and won $60.00 in a craps game. I got back to the ship just before Taps were called letting us know it was time to sleep. It was about 9:45 pm (2145 hours). Taps was at 10:00 pm (2200 hours). I did not have duty the next day, so I stayed up a little later.

There were seventeen of us that slept in the Gunnery office. Every one of us had a place for our cots. We also had our lockers there. That is where I was during the attack when the bombs started dropping.

We had been allowed to sleep in a little longer because we didn`t have to clean the deck anymore. We had a good deal there in the Gunnery office.

In the early morning hours on Sunday, December 7, 1941, at 6:00 am (0600 hours), Reveille was sounded throughout the ship. I remember I got up early. I got up and went to the chow line. I had cream chipped beef on toast with two pieces of bacon and a large glass of milk.

I started a conversation with two other shipmates from the Gunnery office. The buzzing scuttlebutt was about the tension between the United States and Japan. We all were worried about a possible attack. We discussed this for a while.

I went back through the chow line for seconds. I then returned to the Gunnery office to get ready to hit the showers. I was off duty and was going to go on liberty back to Honolulu again. I had to walk all the way forward to turret one to take a shower. I finished my shower and came back down going down through the compartments into turret three.

I was standing in the lower handling room in front of my locker changing my clothes when we heard a load rumbling sound. About that time, the chief turret captain came through a passageway into the bottom of the turret and said, “The Japs are bombing us.”

We all headed for our battle stations. At the same time, the ship was announcing, "General Quarters, General Quarters! This is not a drill! Man your battle stations!" We were unable to be very effective even after we manned our battle stations as we only had fourteen-inch guns.

When I left my locker, I grabbed my wallet which included the $60.00 that I had won the night before playing craps. That was the only thing I saved from my locker. Halfway up, I was on the shell deck where the fourteen-inch projectiles were stored. They each weighed about 1,900 pounds. They were chained together so they would not move.

That is where I was when the ammo magazine blew up. That explosion knocked out the lights, The emergency backup lights came on and they were not very bright. The explosions caused the projectiles to fall down and roll around on the deck.

I made it up to the Gunroom with everyone else. Smoke was really thick. The uniform of the day was a white T shirt with white shorts. The Officers in charge thought the smoke was coming through the sight ports so they made us take off our shirts and stuff them in the sight ports to stop the smoke from entering.

The smoke was actually coming inside the ship from a bomb that had exploded down by turret four. It went through the passageways and up into turret three. By then, the strafing had slowed down and we put our T shirts on again.

They let us go out to the main deck. We took the life rafts off the turrets. The life rafts were wooden and heavy, and we put them in the water to take the wounded off the ship. Most of the wounded came out of the third division compartment. They were burned really badly because they had been wearing just the T shirt and shorts. The flash burns had scalded them. Some of my shipmates were calling out my name, but I could not recognize them because they were so severely burned. We all worked together and put the wounded in life rafts. Then we put them in makeshift beds on the floor.

T deck Lt. Commander Sam Fuqua gave the order to abandon ship. The ship had sunk down a lot and the main deck was level with the water when I stepped on the life raft. I waited to until the fourth raft departed. I stayed behind to help get more wounded off the ship.

A shipmate of mine that was from Oklahoma was trying to convince me to leave the ship. I told him there was work still to be done. I saw him dive off the ship into burning oil. I found out later that he survived by swimming through the burning oily water.

I finally got off the ship on the last boat launch. We headed to Ford Island. We all reported to a bomb shelter. We stayed there overnight and slept on the floor on makeshift beds. They lost my records, naturally. There was no one who seemed to be in charge.

The next day we all made our way to chow and ate really well. We were able to go and borrow uniforms from the Ford Island barracks. We then got to go out on liberty to Honolulu. I met up with other shipmates from my Division. I remember I had a feeling of loss. There was a different feeling in the air that was hard to describe.

We heard that they were looking for volunteers to serve on destroyers. So, we took a motorboat over to the Destroyer base. I was sent to serve on board the U.S.S. Patterson (DD-392) that was just temporary duty.

Three months later, I was transferred to the U.S.S. Aylwin (DD-355) for permanent duty. While serving on board, we were involved in Coral Sea battle and took survivors from the U.S.S. Lexington (CV-2) Aircraft carrier and other ships. After the battle of Coral Sea, we went back to

Pearl Harbor and got supplies and provisions. We stayed overnight then we were off to Midway.

We were involved in the Battle of Midway. We lost a couple of carriers at Midway. After Midway, we went back to Pearl Harbor.

I then was transferred to Washington, DC to go to Electro-hydraulic school. There I learned how to work on 5" 50 caliber guns. After three months of training, I was transferred to the Boston Navy shipyard in South Boston and assigned to U.S.S. Pringle (DD-477), a new destroyer.

We had our shakedown cruise off the coast of Portland, Maine. While finishing up with sea trials our ship got the word to meet up with the Battleship U.S.S. Iowa (BB-61). President Roosevelt was on board the Iowa after he departed his presidential yacht, the U.S.S Potomac at the mouth of the Potomac River. This was in November 1943.

We escorted the President and his presidential party which included The Joint Chiefs of Staff along with their aides to Bermuda. We stayed overnight. We then followed the Iowa across the Mediterranean to rendezvous with a British ship and escorted the Iowa to Yalta for the big meeting. Our ship anchored at Dakkar with three Italian cruisers that had surrendered.

Some natives came down the river and one stood up and yelled, "Anyone from Oklahoma?" There were two of us and this native told us he had lived in Muskogee and went back before the war started. The next morning, we got underway to Sierra Leone to Freetown where we spent four days. We then came back up and picked up the Iowa and escorted her back to New York and finished our shakedown cruise. We went through the Panama Canal to the Pacific in time for the Marshall Islands. We shelled Guam, Tinian and Saipan and were then transferred to Charleston,

South Carolina. While in Charleston, we put the USS Hall, DD-583 in commission.

After the shakedown cruise, we headed back out to the Western Pacific for the Iwo Jima invasion. We landed troops there and stayed until the island was taken. I was the gun captain of number four mount, a five-inch gun. I was in the hatch with binoculars and watching what was going on.

We had a Marine officer on board to tell us where to fire. He told us there were eight hundred pillboxes on the island. I was watching and fired on targets, and I witnessed the second raising of the American flag.

From Iwo Jima, we landed troops on Okinawa and fought there until it was finished. We were there about two months. The Japanese suicide planes were bad. I remember at night we had to fire star shells to keep the beach lit up so the Japs would not get in the foxholes with our troops.

We had two guns on watch at all times. One gun would fire a star shell, and when it just about went out, the other gun would fire a star shell. We kept star shells in the sky all night. We were told those guns would fire five thousand rounds before they had to be taken off and the barrels relined. One of our guns fired over seventeen thousand rounds and another fired fifteen thousand rounds. They fired just as well as when they fired the first round.

They were wasting a lot of money to reline those barrels. At night when we were firing the star shells, something would happen on the beach, and we had to change ammunition. We had a Commodore who was the commander of the destroyer fleet which included forty-six destroyers. There were only six that did not get hit or sunk and we were one of those six.

I think the reason we did not get hit is because our commander on board was sending the ships out on picket duty. This meant they were placed in a friendly position to provide screening and early warning against enemy advance. Every night two destroyers went out on picket duty about twenty-five or thirty miles out toward Japan. They gave us advance notice that the suicide planes were coming. Of course, the suicide planes hit those two ships first. The Alywin, the ship I served on previously was sunk on picket duty. A lot of my shipmates and my friends were killed.

At Okinawa, a number five-gun mount were the guns firing the star shells. I went to the gun and moved them up to number four-gun mount. When they were out, I put the hot shell gloves on and opened the breech. I took the twenty-six pounds of powder and went out on the deck to throw it over the side. It could go off at any time and just as I got out on the deck, they fired a shell and I thought that powder in my hands had exploded. I threw it two or three feet. I went back in the turret and put new powder in. I called the bridge and asked which was safe to fire and they told me. I closed the breech, trained it, fired the gun and everything was fine. When Japan surrendered, we came back to Pearl Harbor.

I have been to Pearl Harbor and the memorial which is located directly over the Arizona.

If you go and visit the memorial, you will see the tallest ring and that is the barbet of turret number three. The barbet is the ring that the turret rotated on. That is the turret I climbed out of and survived.

I received an Honorable discharge from the U.S. Navy in 1948. I married my wife, Marietta on June 23, 1950, in Salinas, California and we started our family.

My wife passed away December 11,2018.

Author's note:

We lost Lonnie Cook on July 31, 2019. It was both an honor and privilege to have known Lonnie Cook.

Fair winds and following seas, Shipmate, friend and Battleship brother.

We now have the watch, Sir. Rest in peace.

Vernon Hand

1919 – 2003

The following paragraphs will tell you how this story came to be in this book and will let you know how important it is to share these stories. I received the following information in response to my post on Facebook:

Good afternoon, Sir! My name is Brad Bagwell. I saw your post on Facebook about your book project, and that is fascinating! I am a Navy veteran of the Cold War, serving on two of the old Knox class frigates in the late 70's and early 80's (USS Blakely, FF-1072 and USS Jesse L. Brown, (FF-1089). I was never stationed in Pearl Harbor, though I did spend two weeks there as a reservist back in the early 90's. I do, however, have a Pearl Harbor Survivor story...of a sort. I have to admit that it is one of the highlights of my life.

When one of my sons was in the fifth grade, he was assigned a project on World War II. He had to 1) interview a veteran, or 2) interview someone who worked in the war industry during that time. There was a third option that I do not recall.

I knew of a gentleman that attended the same church as my family, so I reached out through a mutual acquaintance and arranged a meeting with Mr. Vernon Hand. It turns out that Mr. Hand was Chief Gunner's Mate, United States Navy (ret).

On December 7, 1941, he was a seaman aboard the USS Arizona. Chief Hand invited my son and me into his home, and most graciously and patiently answered any and all questions we asked him.

My son had a prepared list of things to ask, and I reproduced them. I admit that I had goosebumps for the two plus hours we spent with him. Here I was in the presence of living history!

Chief Hand pulled out old scrapbooks, and a shoebox with yellowed newspaper clippings from the day. He said he had never been back to Pearl Harbor and had no desire to go back. His wife had visited there some years prior. He was very open and honest about how he, a humble Christian man, had never been able to forgive the Japanese for what they had done to us, and to his friends.

Chief Hand passed away in 2003. I hope this helps with your book. Thank you for your service, Sir!

Below is an interview with Mr. Vernon Hand. The actual questions are listed with his answers below each question.

What did you do in World War II?

I worked with the guns as a Gunners Mate in the Navy aboard the USS Arizona.

How long had you been in the Navy when the attack on Pearl Harbor occurred?

I had been aboard the USS Arizona about fifteen months before the attack. I ended up serving in the Navy for about nineteen and half years.

What was your job or specialty?

I was a Turret Captain and also stood Helm Watches driving the ship.

Where were you on the morning of December 7, 1941?

I was working topside on the main deck on one of the aircraft catapults.

What was it like to be attacked?

It was a complete shock and surprise.

How long did the attack last?

It lasted about one and a half to two hours. I got off the ship about 9:30 that morning and it was over by then.

Were you injured?

No. Not even a scratch. I was not injured then or any time during the war. I was very lucky. I guess the good Lord wasn't done with me yet.

How many of your friends were injured or killed?

About ninety-five of them. I came aboard in a "draft" of one hundred men. Five of them survived.

How badly was the ship damaged?

The ship sank. The ship took six or seven torpedoes and about the same number of bombs. The torpedoes made the ship, which was about thirty-five thousand tons, rise up out of the water when they hit. One of the bombs went into an ammo magazine and the ship blew up.

What kind of ship was it and what could it do?

It was a battleship. It could sink other ships, do shore bombardment, or shoot at airplanes with its smaller guns. It also carried two small airplanes for recon.

Was the ship able to fight back during the attack?

I don't think so. All the ammunition was stored below deck.

What did you do after the attack?

I went by boat to Ford Island. The boat actually pulled me along in the water while I held on to a towel. I stayed in a bomb shelter all day. That night, I went over to the USS Tennessee. I was very tired.

How many other ships were attacked?

Almost all the ships that were in the harbor, including the battleships.

Did the Japanese attack only the Navy base?

They attacked all of the military bases on Oahu which included Schofield Army Barracks and Hickam Airfield. Everything.

Did you know at first that the attackers were Japanese?

No. I thought they were U.S. Army planes flying in formation until I saw the rising sun on the wings.

Why did they attack?

They wanted to cripple the U.S. Navy in the Pacific Ocean in one strike. They thought our carriers would be there, but they weren't. Without an effective Navy to fight them, they could invade and conquer all the islands in the Pacific and finally invade the United States.

Have you been to the USS Arizona memorial?

No. I never had a strong desire to go there, but my wife has been.

Were you in any other battle in World War II?

I was in six other battles, including the invasion of Iwo Jima.

Do you think Americans remember Pearl Harbor and World War II as they should?

No. Americans are not taught respect for the flag or patriotism anymore.

How did the attack affect your family?

They almost had a funeral for me. They thought I was dead. It was two weeks before I could call home.

FCS1 Paul Author Martin
U.S. Navy
This is a Pearl harbor survivor story as told by Bobby.(@our_Heros_ Headstones)

Paul Martin was born in Salt Lake, Utah in 1915. When Paul was just a young child, he and his family moved to Salida, Colorado. He and his brothers played on one of the Salida High School athletic teams. They won three consecutive State Championships.

In January 1941, Paul enlisted in the United States Navy. After Boot camp and his "A" school training for Fire Control Technician which took 20 weeks to complete, Paul was off to join the fleet.

When Paul joined the fleet, he was assigned to the U.S.S. St. Louis (CL-49). The St. Louis was the eighth of nine Brooklyn class light cruisers and was the fifth ship named after the city of St. Louis, Missouri. The St. Louis was commissioned on May 19, 1939.

Paul rose to the rank of Petty Officer First Class.

The U.S.S. St. Louis was extremely active in World War II earning eleven battle stars. On September 28, 1941, the St. Louis was in dry dock at Pearl Harbor shipyard for routine maintenance. The St. Louis was then moved to Southeast Loch, Berth B-17.

On the early morning of December 7, 1941, Paul was waking up as reveille sounded at 0600 hours (6 A.M.). At 0756 Hours (7:56 A.M.), General Quarters was sounded on the ship which is a signal that all hands aboard a ship must go to battle stations as quickly as possible. Two officers had spotted two low-flying planes, and this was the beginning of the Japanese sneak attack on the Navy.

The St. Louis detached from her mooring dock. She was the only cruiser to make it out to the open sea. She staffed all battery of guns and was able to shoot down several enemy planes.

After the attack, the St. Louis was used for rescue efforts, and is credited with saving numerous lives.

Paul stayed on board the St. Louis throughout the duration of the war and saw heavy battle in the Pacific.

After World War II, Paul was honorably discharged from the U.S. Navy, and he returned to civilian life in Colorado. He continued to be a member in the Navy Ready Reserves.

In 1950 Paul was recalled for active duty again. He served during the Korean War from 1950 to 1952.

Paul met and married his wife, Kathryn, in 1950. They had three children together.

Upon completion of his Naval service, Paul received his college degree and eventually became a teacher.

Paul passed away in 2006 at the age of 90 years old. He and Kathryn are buried next to each other and will rest alongside each other forever.

To U.S. Navy Petty Officer First class Paul A. Martin, the world thanks you!

Paul A. Martin

Doris Miller
October 12, 1919 – November 24, 1943

Doris (Dorie) Miller was born in Waco, Texas. His parents were Connery Miller who worked as a sharecropper and Henrietta Miller. He was born on October 12, 1919, the third of four sons.

The midwife who attended his birth was named Doris. She had wrongly predicted that the baby would be a girl and she and the parents had agreed to name the baby girl Doris. Much to their surprise, they had another boy. That boy still ended up being named Doris, after the midwife. He was given the nickname of Dorie.

In 1938, Dorie attended A.J. Moore high school in Waco, Texas. He played football as a star fullback and was a great athlete. He helped his family work their farm. He wanted to help his family so much that he ended up dropping out of school to go to work as a cook in a local small café in Waco. This was during the Great Depression and times were economically hard on every family. Many were just trying to get by and were struggling to keep their families fed.

In September 1939, less than a month before his twentieth birthday, Dorie joined the United States Navy. His Navy recruiter was located in Dallas, Texas.

Dorie was sent to Norfolk, Virginia for Basic Training (boot camp). After eight weeks of training, Dorie was shipped off to the fleet for assignment. For his first duty station, he reported to the U.S.S. West Virginia BB-48.

On the morning of December 7, 1941, the U.S.S. West Virginia was moored next to the U.S.S. Tennessee BB-43 on Battleship Row located near Ford Island in Pearl Harbor, Hawaii.

On board the U.S. S. West Virginia, reveille which is sounded to wake military personnel was heard at 0600 hours (6:00 AM). Dorie made his way to the bathroom to brush his teeth and splash water in his face to wake up. He then headed to the Galley for breakfast.

The cooks and mess attendants always got to eat before the rest of the crew. It was just one of the fringe benefits of being in food service on board ship.

Shortly before 0800 (8:00 AM), Dorie was collecting dirty laundry from his berthing area which was located below deck on the starboard side of the ship.

When the first bombs hit the U.S.S. West Virginia, the General Quarters (Battle Stations) alarm was sounded throughout the ship's public address system to let the entire crew know the ship was under attack.

Dorie reported to the main deck, and he immediately helped the Captain of the ship, Mervyn Bennion. Captain Bennion was mortally wounded, and Dorie moved him to safety.

Dorie then ran to an unattended anti-aircraft gun and started firing at the enemy planes. This was Dorie's first time to ever shoot these guns and he had never been trained on them. Due to the segregated U.S. Navy, black sailors in the Steward's Navy did not receive weapon training as the white sailors did.

Dorie shot down two to five Japanese planes before being ordered to abandon ship.

On May 27, 1942, Petty Officer Third Class Doris Miller was awarded the Navy Cross for his acts of heroism by the U.S. Navy in a ceremony at Pearl Harbor.

Dorie took leave for Christmas in 1942 and had no idea that it would be the very last time he ever got to see his family and his hometown of Waco, Texas.

Dorie reported to the U.S. S. Liscome Bay ACV-56 which was an escort carrier as a Mess Attendant First Class Petty Officer. The ship was involved in a battle of the Gilbert Islands which is about halfway between Papua New Guinea and Hawaii. Dorie's ship was torpedoed and sunk in the Pacific Ocean. He was killed in action.

There is a Doris Miller Memorial located in his hometown of Waco, Texas as recognition of his selfless courage. On June 3, 1972, the U.S.S. MillerFF-1091 was named and commissioned in his honor.

On January 20, 2020, the United States Navy announced the newest Gerald R. Ford Class Super Aircraft Carrier would be named the U.S.S. Doris Miller CVN-81 and dedicated to Doris Miller.

Much respect, Sir.

THE FORGOTTEN SURVIVORS

THE CHILDREN WHO WITNESSED PEARL HARBOR

LeRoy Bosanko

On December 7, 1941, shortly before 8 A.M. my father was walking near the water's edge holding me in his arms in Pearl City, located on Oahu, Hawaii. I was only fifteen months old at the time.

Some planes were flying up above our heads. We witnessed the U.S.S. Utah (BB-31) moored near Ford Island. A Japanese plane dropped a torpedo that hit the Utah on the port (left) side of the ship. We saw the Utah capsize and roll over and sink.

We lived in Pearl City. My Dad was shot in his left arm while holding me in his right arm. He watched what he thought was a military exercise. He then reported to the U.S.S. Argonne (AS-10) and my mother, Ellen Marie, and I fled to some local caves waiting for the expected troop landings for about a week. Six months later, we returned stateside.

Obviously, I was very young at the time of attack and most of what I remember most likely came from my mother who told me the stories.

My father's name was Leroy Osborne Bosanko and he was born in 1915. He joined the United States Navy in 1934. He went to Basic training (boot camp) in San Diego, California at RTC/NTC. He served on Board U.S.S. Argonne (AS-10). His Navy rank and rating (Job) was a MM (Machinist Mate.

In the Navy, a Machinist mate's job is to be responsible for operating and maintaining the ship propulsion machinery. That machinery includes aligning piping systems for oil, water, air, and steam.

My Father retired from the Navy in 1956, as a Chief Warrant Officer 4.

Some facts concerning the Battleship Utah:

The U.S.S. Utah (BB-31) was a 21,825-ton Florida class battleship. She was built at Camden, New Jersey and commissioned in August 1911 and operated in the Atlantic during her years of service. The Utah made a voyage to the Mediterranean in 1913. She also played a role in the Vera Cruz incident. The Utah continued to serve in the Atlantic throughout World war I.

In September through November 1918, the Utah was based out of Southern Ireland to provide a force of protection for Allied convoys as they reached the British Isles.

Post war, the Utah operated along the east coast shores and in the Caribbean. Then she was assigned to European waters during 1921-22.

In 1924-25, the Utah made a good-will visit to South America. In 1925, she went through an extremely complete modernized makeover. In 1928 she went to the South Atlantic to transport President-elect Herbert Hoover on his homeward bound leg of his South American tour.

In 1931 the Utah was converted to a radio-controlled target ship and was re-designated (AG-16). She spent the rest of her service in this role. She had additional duties as an anti-aircraft gunnery training ship starting mid 1930`s.

In 1941, the Utah was outfitted with some additional guns to help enhance her gunnery training. On December 7, 1941, the Utah was stationed at Pearl Harbor, Hawaii. She was moored at berth F-11 after have completing another round of anti-aircraft gunnery training Just shortly before 0800 (8 A.M.). The USS Utah BB-31 (AG-16) was hit by two Japanese torpedoes on her port side (left) of the ship which caused her to capsize and roll over and sink in the shallow harbor.

There was a crew of one thousand and one officers and enlisted men. A total of fifty-eight crew members died. About four hundred sixty-one crew members were able to abandon ship and swim to safety. Only four of those killed were ever recovered or identified.

To the officers and crew, we thank you for your service and dedication to your country, Shipmates.

Much respect.

JANET JONES

This is the survivor story of Janet Jones who was eight years old in 1941. She was the daughter of Stephine Jones who was a Marine Corps Lance Corporal (E-3). He was stationed at Pearl City, Hawaii on the Island of Oahu. His military post was at The Marine Corps, Air Station, Ewa, Oahu. He was attached to the Marine Aircraft Group 21(Mag-21) and served under the command of Lieutenant Colonel Claude A. Larkin.

These are her words:

On the morning of December 7, 1941, my father left our Housing Quarters early that morning to report for duty at the Airfield. I remember it was still dark outside when he left. My mother, Judy, was making me and my little sister, Suzie, pancakes that morning. I helped my mother take care of my little sister as she was only five years old. After we ate breakfast, our mom took us for a walk by the water's edge. The sun was just rising up on the over the horizon, I remember just how beautiful it really was. My mom said she had an uneasy feeling that our Dad was in some sort of danger, and she didn`t know why. We took a rest from walking and sat down.

Suzy and I were playing in the sand. From a distance we heard a load rumble sound coming from the air. We then saw several airplanes in the sky. I thought it was strange that the planes didn`t look like the planes where my Dad was stationed. I remember they had a big red dot on them.

We then heard the explosions and a really big fire ball. My mom told me it came from one of the Navy ships in the Harbor. I still remember how the sky got so dark with black smoke. My mom took us by the hands and took us to some nearby caves for safety.

I remember all three of us were crying with all the confusion. We were really worried and concerned for our Dad's safety. While we were safe, the Airfield was under full attack. My Dad and other Marines took fire from the Japanese and returned fire with machine guns.

My Dad sustained a gunshot to his right shoulder. Later, we were able to reunite with him at the Base Hospital.

That day forever changed our lives.

Selchickl "Chick" Takara

The following is a Japanese/American child's story from survivor Seikichl "Chick" Takara.

In 1941, Chick Takara, a Japanese/American was twelve years old. He lived with his parents and five siblings in Honolulu, Hawaii. He was born in 1929 in Honolulu, Hawaii.

On the morning of December 7, 1941, Chick and his brother were allowed to get a job at a local restaurant which was located midtown Honolulu. His parents allowed Chick and his brother to work on Sundays to help his family put food on the table. Chick said, "We all did our part."

His father worked as cook. He told me if I wanted to eat three square meals a day, I needed to learn how to cook like he did. It was usually slow for customers on Sunday mornings at the restaurant. My brother and I were hired to wash dishes.

Pearl Harbor

On the morning of December 7, 1941, it was not really busy at all. I remember that a taxicab driver came to have a cup of coffee before 8 A.M. He said something to us to try and get our attention. He said for us to go and look at the harbor. He said, "It looks like the U.S. Navy is engaged in military exercises and using real ammunition."

I remember my brother and I climbed a ladder to get a better view, towards the direction of Pearl Harbor Navy Base. We saw hundreds of grey and white powder puffs all over the sky. Our boss told us to go home. We took a trolley car for a thirty-minute ride. Then we headed for our home in the tenements at a brisk sprint while yelling, "This is war, Mommy!"

The streets were quiet and empty that morning except for sounds of explosions coming from the harbor. At approximately 8:10 A.M. fires broke out on McCully Street and at Lunalilo Elementary school.

I remember seeing my Mom and a neighbor standing outside talking and they were both holding laundry in their arms. The neighbor turned and went back upstairs for the rest of her laundry. A big gray streak shot across the sky as with a loud boom, a bomb hit the building with our neighbor still inside.

I was too terrified to scream. I was frozen in terror. The fire spread fast. My father told all six of his kids to hold hands to keep us safe. The plan was for all of us to walk over to the nearby stadium and sit together on the fifty-yard line. We thought we would all die together.

The Japanese American community comprised at least 38% of the people living in Hawaii in 1940. The Principal of the local Japanese school, a large part of the Japanese American community and a group of us stayed for weeks at the school as shelter.

We slept on tatami mats that were used at one time by young Japanese girls who sat on them and learned how to sew kimonos. The school's gymnasium was used as a clearinghouse for Japanese residents, and we were then declared enemy aliens. We were ordered to turn in and surrender our belongings to them. All radios, binoculars, and weapons.

When my family was allowed to try to salvage any belongings from our home, we found it had been completely destroyed. We found a bunch of coins that were melted and fused together, a memento of the tragedy that we still have today.

That was eighty-one years ago, and I am now ninety-three years old. I still remember December 7, 1941, like it was just yesterday. This tragic event forever changed my life and forever molded the way I am today.

I had always been artistic, however, my parents could not afford to send me to Art school. One of my schoolteachers took an interest in me and paid the cost for me to attend Art school.

STORIES FROM FAMILIES OF PEARL HARBOR SURVIVORS

FREDERICK (FRED) HENLEY FRANKS

February 27, 1915 – June 15, 1963

Shared by Shannon Cooper

Frederick (Fred) Henley Franks was my grandfather. In our family, he was affectionately known as "Paw Paw." He was born on February 15, 1915, in Meeke, Louisiana which is located in Rapides Parish. The state of Louisiana uses Parish instead of naming them Counties. This is due to the fact that Louisiana was officially Roman Catholic under rule of both France and Spain. The boundaries dividing the territories coincided with church parishes.

Fred and his family moved to Bunkie, Louisiana which is located in Avoyelles Parish. That is where he grew up.

In 1929, Fred attended Terrebonne High School in Terrebonne Parish which is in the town of Houma, Louisiana. Their school mascot is Isa the Tiger. Fred was on the high school football team and played defensive end and tackle on the Varsity team.

He graduated with the class of 1933 with honors as the Valedictorian. He earned a full athletic scholarship to Louisiana State University located in Baton Rouge, Louisiana. His major course of study was Seminary Religious Ministries.

Fred also participated in the school's Reserve Officers Training Corps (ROTC).

On February 19, 1935, Fred married the love of his life, Ruby Pearl Free. They were married in Marthaville, Louisiana in a small, cozy ceremony with family and a few close friends attending.

In 1937, Fred graduated with a bachelor's degree in Religious Studies (Theology). After college, he answered a call to preach at a small Methodist in Bunkie, Louisiana called Fairview Church. He also worked on a dairy farm located close to Bunkie.

On October 16, 1940, Fred registered for the draft at his local post office in Bunkie. While he was finishing filling out his card, a young, ambitious Navy recruiter named Charley Sigga entered the post office. Charley was there to mail some recruit applications to the main recruiting office. Fred and Charley struck up a conversation and Fred decided to join the Navy Reserve program.

Three days later, he was off to the Armed Services Induction Center in Shreveport, Louisiana. Then he was off to Basic Training (Boot Camp) in Great Lakes Naval Recruit Training Center in Great Lakes, Illinois which is just outside of Chicago, Illinois.

After eight weeks of training, Fred was offered the choice of going back to his reserve unit or going on active duty. Fred wanted to serve his country. After a long and difficult phone call home, his wife agreed with him and he went on active duty.

At that point, Fred was sent to his "A" school for the rate (job) of storekeeper. Storekeepers in the United States Navy are responsible for maintaining ship or company military supplies. They are also in charge of purchasing ship supplies, equipment, and consumables. These are obtained through the Federal Stock System. Fred was sent to the storekeeper's "A" school at the Naval Air Station in Meridian, Mississippi for forty days of technical training.

In addition to working as the ship's storekeeper, my grandfather also served as a Navy barber and cut the sailors' hair.

After completing "A" school, Fred took thirty days of leave (vacation) to get everything all worked out with his family.

In August 1941, Fred was flown out to meet his ship in the fleet. On board the U.S.S. Pennsylvania BB-38 Battleship, he reported as an SK2 Second Class Petty Officer. His ship was off the coast of Panama where she engaged in fleet tactics and battle practice maneuvers. Then on to the Caribbean for more battle training and exercises.

On December 6, 1941, the U.S.S. Pennsylvania was in drydock, Berth F-3 in the Pearl Harbor, Hawaii shipyard. It was located away from Battleship Row and on the south side of Ford Island.

Fred remembered coming back from Liberty call around 2030 hours (8:30 pm) after a Saturday night on the town in Honolulu, Hawaii. After talking to his Chief Petty Officer Joseph Newman about an upcoming ship's order and delivery, he went to his bunk (S-3 Berthing area) located two decks below the main deck on the starboard side of the ship. Fred was looking forward to Sunday morning because they were being treated to omelets they could order.

At 0600 hours (6 am) Sunday morning, reveille was sounded throughout the ship in those early morning hours on December 7, 1941. Fred took a quick shower which was common practice on board ship in an effort to conserve water supplies. He then went to the Mess deck for that incredible Navy chow, some of the best in the fleet. Fred sat down to a western omelet with peppers, onions, ham and cheese made with two large eggs. He also had hash browns, orange juice and a large glass of milk.

Fred sat next to fellow Storekeeper Third Class Luis Gardner who had a wife at home in Missouri. They both commented on how homesick they were. After breakfast, they went to the Storekeepers office to work on an inventory list of the ship's supplies.

At approximately 0800 hours (8 am), a loud explosion was heard coming from the harbor close to where their ship was drydocked. The ship announced over the public address system, "General quarters. General quarters. Man your battle stations. This is not a drill."

Fred and Chief Petty Officer Newman reported to their battle station located next to each other. At 0802 to 0805 (8:02 am to 8:05 am), Fred and Chief Petty Officer Newman were posted on two anti-aircraft guns (76 MM-23 Caliber) and started firing at Japanese planes.

All anti-aircraft batteries were rapidly brought into action. There were attacks by enemy planes which were releasing torpedoes. Three planes came in low from port beam. One Japanese plan was seen to burst into flames about two thousand yards off the starboard bow. The ship was hit with a bomb strike that killed the crew that was manning a 5" gun mount.

The bulk of the damage was sustained by flying shrapnel and debris from the two destroyers, U.S.S. Cassin (DD-372) located in drydock F-2 and U.S.S. Downes (DD-375) located in drydock F-1. The U.S.S. Shaw (DD-373) was hit with a bomb and exploded. Dive bombing attacks on Hickman Airfield continued.

Around 0830 (8:30 am), the U.S.S. Nevada (BB-36) was able to break away from its moor and make it out to the open sea. It was the only battleship to depart Pearl Harbor and use rapid fire to shoot down several enemy planes.

A one-thousand-pound torpedo tube struck the U.S.S. Pennsylvania forecastle. After the battle was over, the U.S.S. Pennsylvania had fifteen crew members killed including the Executive Officer. Another fourteen crew members were missing and thirty-eight were injured.

Fred and Chief Petty Officer Newman assisted in the search for survivors. Both of them were awarded the Navy Cross for their acts of heroism.

Fred stayed on board the U.S.S. Pennsylvania for the remainder of his active duty. He then returned to his wife in Louisiana.

He continued to preach at a small church in Marthaville, Louisiana until he died of a heart attack on June 15, 1963, at forty-eight years of age.

I really have no memories of my Paw Paw because he died when I was only one year and ten months old. I only know what I was told.

I was able to tell his story because my Maw Maw, his wife, kept a diary and saved all of Fred's letters. I was told that I was his "shadow" and we were inseparable. I was his "little buddy." He bought me a little sailor suit.

Little did he know that I would follow in his footsteps and join and serve in the United States Navy. I also served on a battleship.

Like Paw Paw, I also have a bachelor's degree in Religious studies and have worked as a Youth Minister for the Church of Christ. I was a Chaplain for the Veterans of Foreign Wars (VFW) Post 1195 in Okmulgee, Oklahoma and also taught Sunday school classes. I was born in Shreveport, Louisiana.

Thank you for your service, Paw Paw.

ALBERT GEORGE MARSTON

Shared by Shannon Cooper

Albert George Marston is a member of my family. In fact, he is my great uncle. We called him Uncle Al. He joined the United States Army on June 14, 1940 in Boston, Massachusetts. He was stationed on the island of Oahu in Hawaii at Wheeler Army Airfield.

Wheeler Army Airfield, also known as Wheeler Field, was a primary target and the site of the first attack on December 7, 1941 which led up to the attack on Pearl Harbor. The Japanese attacked the airfield to prevent the numerous planes that were there from going airborne and engaging the Japanese planes.

My great uncle was at Wheeler Field during the attack and kept detailed notes of his experience. He did not go into much detail about the attack, and I assume he had a lot of traumas that he did not wish to re-live through writing about it.

In June of 1941, he met a Lieutenant (Lt.) in the Army Air Force who was the pilot of a B-24 known as "Dogpatch Express." His name was Lt. Deasy. There is a book about this plane called *Finish Forty and Home* and was written by the son of one of the crewmen. There is a passage that describes my Uncle Al as very resentful about what happened at Pearl

Harbor and that he wanted to avenge the many friends he lost during the attack. However, his orders prevented him from pulling Guard Duty on Oahu.

Against regulations, he kept a rifle and bandoliers of ammunition next to his bunk every night. He swore he would never be caught off guard like he and many others were on that fateful day.

Lt. Deasy had taken a liking to my Uncle Al. When the B-24s arrived at Hickham Field, they were retro-fitted with a belly turret. With the addition of a message turret, there was also a need for a new Gunner. Lt. Deasy knew just the man for the job.

Lt. Deasy had my Uncle Al's orders re-assigned to the Army Air Corps, After a couple of months of practice runs and submarine patrols off the shores of Oahu, the men of Dogpatch Express would get their first taste of combat.

On April 18, 1943, the 42nd Bombardment squadron departed for Fanafuti, one of the most populated islands in the west-central Pacific Ocean. The bomber crews spent the night at Funafuti preparing for the first mission the next morning to Nauru, an island country northeast of Australia.

The bomber crews spent the night at Funafuti preparing for the first mission the next morning.

MORE INFORMATION ON THIS LATER FROM *UNBROKEN BY PHIL SCARCE.*

Once the men returned to Funafuti, they immediately went to rest in their cots waiting to fall asleep while trying to wrap their heads around the concept that they had twenty-four more missions to complete before they could be rotated back home. The Japanese raided Funafuti that night.

My uncle, having already experienced a raid by the Japanese, sprang into action. He commanded the enlisted men of his crew to take cover in a crater. They were barely missed by a Japanese bomb. A fire extinguisher flew into their crater and landed between the legs of Elmer Johnson, the Belly Turret Gunner. The men were certainly shaken up!

After the "Green Hornet" which carried Louis Zamparini on board went missing, Lt. Deasy's crew was assigned to the search mission. As depicted in "Unbroken," the search mission failed and Zamparini was not located. The crew continued to fly missions against the Japanese at Wake Island, Tarawa, Maloelap, Kawajalein and Eniwaytok. My great uncle shot down eight zeroes during all these missions, far surpassing the average of two kills and the life expectancy of a Tail Gunner.On December 21, 1943, Lt. Deasy volunteered my great uncle to serve on a crew whose Tail Gunner had been killed on their previous mission. The B-24 he flew was "Thar She Blows."

"Dogpatch Express" would also be flying on this mission, however, with an entirely different crew than the crew my great uncle flew with on that plane. After making their bombing run and making their turn for home, the number four engine on the "Dogpatch Express" was feathered and began to fall behind the rest of the formation. The other bombers slowed down to give fire support to help fend off the zeroes who were now swarming the wounded bomber. However, this was in vain. "Dogpatch Express" was in rough shape. The cockpit and nose gunner position windows were now covered in blood. My great uncle watched from "Thar She Blows" as his maiden plane, the "Dogpatch Express" hit the water and exploded. All hands were lost.

My great uncle, Albert George Marston, rotated home in February of 1944 and was discharged in Boston, Massachusetts on September 5, 1945.

www.ingramcontent.com/pod-product-compliance
Ingram Content Group UK Ltd.
Pitfield, Milton Keynes, MK11 3LW, UK
UKHW021912190726
13853UKWH00002B/635